Economic Security:

Neglected Dimension of National Security?

Edited by Sheila R. Ronis

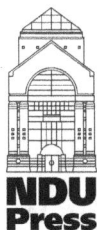

PUBLISHED FOR THE
CENTER FOR STRATEGIC CONFERENCING
INSTITUTE FOR NATIONAL STRATEGIC STUDIES
BY NATIONAL DEFENSE UNIVERSITY PRESS
WASHINGTON, D.C.

NDU Press
2011

Published by Books Express Publishing
Copyright © Books Express, 2012
ISBN 978-1-78039-663-7

Books Express publications are available from all good retail and online booksellers. For
publishing proposals and direct ordering please contact us at: info@books-express.com

Contents

Preface

Five years ago, I had the privilege of conducting a study as a consultant to the U.S. House of Representatives Small Business Committee. Congress asked me, as a systems scientist, to look at a number of defense industrial base issues and their national security implications. The Nation is not well prepared to plan for or establish policy or "grand" strategy in a holistic or long-term sense, and the national security implications of that shortcoming remain very disturbing. I recommended the establishment of a center in the Executive Office of the President for "whole of government" and interagency "foresight capability and grand strategy development" and execution, along with an interagency committee of Congress to have oversight responsibility for the center because the Nation has no means to do this.

Then, in my work with the Project on National Security Reform over the last few years, the Vision Working Group that I led recommended the establishment of a Center for Strategic Analysis and Assessment to provide the mechanism to conduct foresight studies and the development of the grand strategies that would follow—the kind of studies that would look at an entire system, such as the economy and its relationship to national security.

At the end of World War II, General George C. Marshall said, "We are now concerned with the peace of the entire world, and the peace can only be maintained by the strong." But how does the United States remain strong? What does that mean in a world of globalization? And how do we even define what national security is in such a complex and interdependent world? Can we survive, let alone remain a superpower, if we no longer control any means of production? If we remain a major debtor nation? If we continue our dependence on unstable countries for our energy supplies? If we invest insufficient amounts of our resources in research and development, science and technology? Or if we perceive the training and education of people as a cost as opposed to an investment?

Recently, I spoke about the national security implications of a downturn in the economy and the auto industry to some colleagues in Detroit. They said, "What are you talking about? What does the economy have to do with national security?" Most people in our country equate national security with military readiness, homeland defense, and generally protecting American interests at home and abroad. And they would be right, but not entirely. National security has other dimensions. It is a broad description of the elements in our society that make it "secure," and that goes much further than providing for "a common defense." It can include *anything* that adds to the strength of the Nation. It is about being strong in the sense General Marshall intended.

Historically, *national security* includes the strength of our nation's infrastructure, the foundation upon which the continuous growth of our society depends. This includes our strong societal and moral codes, the rule of law, stable government, social, political, and economic institutions, and leadership. Also included are our nation's schools and educational programs to ensure a knowledgeable citizenry and lifelong learning—a must for a democracy. Our nation's strength also requires investments in science, engineering, research and development, and technological leadership. We cannot be strong without a viable way to power our cities, feed ourselves, and move from one place to another. Most of all, a strong economy is an essential ingredient of a global superpower. Without it, we will lose our superpower status, and quickly.

National security must include a healthy market-based economy, with a strong base of globally competitive products and services that produce jobs. This economy must include sound government policies to promote responsible choices and reduce our debt, and grand strategies for energy and environmental sustainability, science and technology leadership (at least in some areas), human capital capabilities, manufacturing, and the industrial base. And these are not the only components.

National security goes to the very core of how we define who we are as a people and a free society. It concerns how we view our world responsibilities.

Economic security is a major element of national security, even as borders are less important than ever. No matter how we look at national security, there can be no question of the need to include the economic viability of our nation. Without capital, there is no business; without business, there is no profit; without profit, there are no jobs. And without jobs, there are no taxes, and there is no military capability.

The viability of a nation's industrial infrastructure, which provides jobs for its people, creates and distributes wealth, and leverages profits, is essential. Without jobs, the quality of peoples' lives deteriorates to a point where society itself can disintegrate. It can also lead to strife on many different levels. As a nation, we need to find a strategy to deal with this, and we will discuss the ideas of expeditionary economics. But poverty is not only a problem in Third World countries. It can occur at home, too—especially during a deep recession. No community, local or global, can sustain indefinitely whole populations of "haves" and "have nots." And that gap is now growing within the United States.

There is no question that a part of the infrastructure of a nation must include a sound economy. It was the relative deterioration of the Japanese and German economies that led those nations into World War II. Poverty around the world is a global systemic issue that frequently can and does lead to political instability. But we cannot help others if we cannot help ourselves, and our current economic crisis is a warning.

National security is societal, political, and economic strength. In today's world, national security for a superpower is meaningless without a strong military capability as well. The sovereignty and security of the United States, and the protection of its citizens and property around the world, remain the bedrock of national security. The execution of U.S. national security strategy is conducted in a highly volatile global environment characterized by quantum changes in technology; unprecedented social, economic, and political interdependencies; broadened opportunities to foster democratic principles; and allegiances and alliances frequently founded on interests other than traditional nationalism.

Understanding the complex systems nature of national security and why the economy is a part of the equation is crucial. The world is a very small place, and world peace may depend upon our ability to understand and articulate these issues—and in particular to recognize the importance of the economic element of national power.

—Sheila R. Ronis

Introduction

> We must renew the foundation of America's strength. In the long run, the welfare of the American people will determine America's strength in the world, particularly at a time when our own economy is inextricably linked to the global economy. Our prosperity serves as a wellspring for our power. It pays for our military, underwrites our diplomacy and development efforts, and serves as a leading source of our influence in the world.
>
> —*The National Security Strategy of the United States,*
>   May 2010

On August 24–25, 2010, the National Defense University held a conference titled *Economic Security: Neglected Dimension of National Security?* The conference explored the economic element of national power. Often ignored and misunderstood in relation to national security, the economy has been taken for granted for years, but its strength is the foundation of national security. Over 2 days, several keynote speakers and participants in six panel discussions explored the complexity surrounding this subject and examined the major elements that, interacting as a system, define the economic component of national security.

As the Nation begins to understand the imperative of putting its problem-solving apparatus into a global systemic context, that framework was used to explore the topic because, as Albert Einstein said, "We cannot solve problems by using the same kind of thinking we used when we created them." And the linear solution sets we once used to solve simplistic problems are of little value in a world of complex systems.

This conference was designed around a systemic framework that could be used to develop a grand strategy surrounding the Nation's economy as a subsystem of national security. The panels and keynote presentations looked at the economic element of national power from different system views. Those views—including the role of debt, the government, industrial capability, energy, science, technology, and human capital—create a systemic view of what could be done to improve an understanding of the economic element of national power. Selected papers from the conference that represent these views comprise this volume.

Chapter one is a transcript of the comments made by opening keynote speaker David Walker. He contends that if the economic element of national power is neglected and misunderstood, nothing will be more dangerous to the Nation than the national debt and its unintended consequences for generations to come. His arguments are alarming and are critical for policymakers and every citizen to understand. He provides a common-sense approach to getting the Nation's financial house in order.

America's role in the world is based on its military and economic prowess and capability. In chapter two, John Morton traces the historical roots of the economy and its role in enabling the superpower status of the Nation. He also proposes that the United States needs an economic grand strategy and describes the road ahead.

No 21st-century economy can be secured without a steady supply of energy. Without adequate energy to power contemporary civilization, there is no security at all. In chapter three, Keith Cooley explains his approach to an energy plan, which includes a grand strategy that, if enacted, will support the Nation's future.

In chapter four, Louis Infante offers his approach to energy security. His National Energy Security Initiative describes a specific model that the Nation could use to manage the complexities of its entire energy system. This initiative would include mechanisms to improve the research and development policymaking decisions and strategies to make them real.

How can a nation be an economic or military superpower without a plan to ensure it has people with the right knowledge and capabilities throughout its society? In chapter five, Myra Shiplett and her team eloquently address this complex set of issues and how the United States will be well served only if its schools can produce individuals who can compete in a sophisticated and globally competitive 21st-century world.

It is probably impossible for the United States to have a robust economy and remain a superpower if its companies lose their ability to be innovative. In chapter six, Carmen Medina explores the many issues that surround what it means to have innovation as a major element of a nation's economy.

Chapter One

We the People: Keeping the Economy and the Nation Strong

David M. Walker

When I became the seventh Comptroller General of the United States, I was shocked to find out when I assumed office in 1998 that the agency that I headed, the Government Accountability Office (GAO), had been in business since 1921 and had no integrated, forward-looking, and outcome-based strategic plan. Now, there are some Federal agencies that are in the same category today that have been in business a lot longer. But what I was even more shocked to find out is that the United States, which has been in business since 1789 as a constitutional republic, still has no strategic, integrated, forward-looking, and outcome-based strategic plan. It is an outrage and an issue we must address.

As a result, we spend a lot of time dealing with immediate needs. We also spend a lot of time focusing on how much money we are going to spend and how much in tax preferences we are going to give. We do not focus enough on what goals and objectives we are trying to achieve, what works, what does not work, what is affordable, and what is sustainable. This exercise has to consider not just today but macro trends and challenges that are affecting us and everyone else in the world and their implications for tomorrow.

We put such a plan in place at GAO, and it is the closest thing that exists to a strategic plan for the Federal Government, but the GAO is in the legislative branch. So we need one for the executive branch. It needs to be led by the OMB (Office of Management and Budget), and hopefully, eventually it will be.

But I can tell you that when you look at performance, you have to look at three dimensions. First, how are we doing based upon our desired outcomes and our key objectives? Second, are we getting better, or are we getting worse? And third and very importantly, ask a question that the United States rarely asks: "How do we compare to our competitor groups or comparator groups?"

If we answered these questions, we would find that while we are above average in many things, we are below average in too many things, and the things that we are below average in are, in many cases, leading indicators with regard to what our future economy is going to be like, what our future position in the world is going to be, and what our future standard of living at home will be. Things like savings, critical infrastructure, investments in basic research, educational outcomes, and healthcare outcomes are key leading indicators, and in all of these areas, we are *below average for an industrialized nation.*

We have rested on our past success too long. We have rampant myopia, tunnel vision, and self-interest. It has reached epidemic proportions in the halls of Congress and in Washington, DC. We need policy, operational, and political reforms, and we need them soon because we have a dysfunctional constitutional republic. If we do not take steps to keep our economy strong for both today and tomorrow, our national security, international standing, standard of living, and even our domestic tranquility will suffer over time. That is the bottom line.

Let me provide you with some context. Today, we have very large short-term deficits—$1.4 trillion plus. Debt is mounting at a rapid rate, and we now have about $13.4 trillion in total debt subject to the debt-ceiling limit. That is a matter of concern, and it is the number-two issue among the American people, only behind the economy and jobs.

While the American people are rightfully concerned about our current debt, it is only the tip of the iceberg, but what threatens the ship of state and our collective future is the part of the iceberg below the water that is represented by off-balance-sheet obligations—tens of trillions in unfunded promises that do not represent deficits today but will represent deficits and debt tomorrow. They represent the true threat to the ship of state.

Even after the economy recovers, even after unemployment is down, even after the "wars" are over—and I put that in quotes because Congress has not declared war since World War II—even after the temporary tax cuts have expired, and even after the financial services and housing crises have long passed, this country faces large, known, and growing structural deficits due to known demographic trends and rising healthcare costs. This enormous problem requires solutions now because our foreign lenders are starting to get nervous and the situation will only get worse absent meaningful reform actions.

The Federal Government has grown dramatically since its founding. In 1800, 11 years after the founding of the Republic, it represented

2 percent of the U.S. economy. This year, it represents 25 percent, which is above the recent average of 21 percent. But if we do not reform our existing entitlement programs and other aspects of government, it will represent about 40 percent of the economy by 2040, and that does not count state and local governments.

The composition of the budget has changed dramatically in the last four decades. Forty years ago, it was dominated by defense at 42 percent. Today, it is dominated by social insurance programs, which grow faster than inflation and grow faster than the economy even when the economy is growing. Forty years ago, when Congress came to town, they got to decide how 62 percent of the budget would be spent, of which today defense is about half of the discretionary budget. Now they decide how about 38 percent gets spent, and if we continue on our status quo, do nothing, let-it-ride policy, it will go down to 18 percent by 2040. This obviously is an imprudent and unsustainable course.

Interestingly, those of you who are scholars of history and the Constitution will find that every enumerated responsibility envisioned by the Founding Fathers for the Federal Government under the Constitution is in discretionary spending, every single one, and discretionary spending is what is getting squeezed. If you look at what has happened in the last 9½ years, our debt has more than doubled, and worse, we do not like to count all of our debt. There is a little creative accounting going on.

There are two kinds of debt: the debt held by the public, and that debt that we owe to Social Security, Medicare, and other trust funds. That debt is also backed by the full faith and credit of the United States Government. It is guaranteed as to principal and interest. It will be honored, but the Federal Government does not want to call it a liability. It wants to tell people who are covered under Social Security and Medicare that they can count on it, and I think you can, but our current accounting treatment is wrong and it should change.

This situation has resulted in understating our true deficits and our true debt to GDP (gross domestic product) for many years, and as far as I know, we are the only country that has so-called trust funds because ours are ones that you can't trust, and they are not funded.

If you look at the last consolidated financial statements of the United States, which were issued earlier this year, as of the end of September 30, 2009, the last fiscal year end, you will find that the total liabilities and unfunded promises primarily for Medicare and Social

Security, the total of the liabilities and unfunded promises, have more than tripled since the year 2000—$62 trillion—and most of this is off the balance sheet.

How much is $62 trillion? It is over $200,000 per person. It is over $500,000 per household. Believe it or not, median household income in the United States is $50,000 a year. So that means that under our status quo, do nothing, let-it-ride path, the typical American household has a second or third mortgage equal to ten times their annual household income, but there is no house backing this mortgage, and the American people do not even know about it.

If you look at deficits and surpluses since 1800, you will find that we have had a long-standing tradition in this country of not running large deficits unless we were at war, a declared war, or we faced great economic challenges, such as the Great Depression or a recession.

But within the last several decades, this country became addicted to deficits and debt and conspicuous consumption. Economists changed from trying to have a balanced budget over the economic cycle, to a point where they said, "Well, let us try to achieve no more than the growth of the economy over a cycle," such that it became acceptable to run deficits of 2 to 3 percent of GDP, even in good times, and times of peace.

The result of that is, you changed the standard. Then what happens when you are in a recession? What happens when you are at war, whether it is declared or undeclared? What happens when you have a national emergency or non–business cycle challenge, a crisis like the housing and financial services meltdown? Deficits of 10 percent of GDP plus. We have lost our metrics. We have lost our way. We have strayed from the principles and values that this country was founded on, including thrift, savings, limited debt, and stewardship, and that needs to change.

Now, what about Social Security? Well, it was running surpluses for a lot of years, and every dime of that surplus was spent for other government operating expenses and replaced with a nonmarketable bond, but those days are over. Social Security is running a deficit now, primarily because of the recession and more people retiring early, and it is going to be in a permanent deficit position within about 5 years, adding to our fiscal challenges rather than reducing them.

What about the future? If we tax at historical levels, 18.3 percent of GDP, which is the green line, and if we do not reform government, this is what the future will look like: the fastest growing expense will be interest on the Federal debt; the second fastest growing Federal expense will be out-of-control healthcare costs, which are still out of control despite the latest healthcare bill. And they are eating everybody's lunch, including the Defense Department's.

And what about debt to GDP? The only time in the history of the United States that we had public debt over 60 percent of GDP was at the end of World War II. But guess what? We got something for that. We defeated the Axis powers, we saved the free world, we avoided attack on the continental United States, and after World War II, we were over 50 percent of the global economy, demographics were working in our favor, and the dollar was as good as gold.

So what did we do? We did a number of things to try to help rebuild the Axis powers and other nations that had experienced mass destruction, in order to stimulate global demand. We did a number of things to invest in our people through the GI Bill and our infrastructure through the highway system. We did a number of things to try to help maintain sound fiscal policy, and we obviously grew the economy very fast, because we dominated the global economy.

Those days are over. We are still a superpower, but we will not be the only superpower forever. That status is temporary. We are still the leading nation on Earth, but we are one of a number of important nations on Earth. And we have to recognize reality, not continue to live on our past successes. We have to start focusing on the future and on results. Guess what? Today, our debt to GDP is above 60 percent for only the second time in the history of the United States, and it's rising rapidly. If you counted the debt that we owe to Social Security and Medicare, it is over 90 percent of GDP.

And what about Greece, Italy, Portugal, Spain, Ireland, the United Kingdom? If you look at appropriate metrics, which are total Federal, state, and local debt held by the public—again, ignoring the trust fund debt—if you just look at that, according to a 2010 International Monetary Fund report, we are already worse than Spain, we are already worse than Ireland, we are already worse than the United Kingdom, and we are within 10 years of being where Greece is today.

What about that debt that we owe to Social Security and Medicare? If you count that, we are within 3 years of being where Greece is today. We are not Greece, but Greece used to be the greatest civilization in the history of mankind. Greece is the cradle of democracy, and ruled most of the world during Alexander's time. Unfortunately, we have more rope because we have over 60 percent of the global reserve currency, but we do not have unlimited rope, and we are not exempt from the laws of prudent finance.

We are a safe haven in times of uncertainty, but that is temporary. We need to wake up; we need to recognize reality. We need to start making tough choices before people lose confidence in our ability to put our own financial house in order, because if we don't get our act together, we will have our own debt crisis. The result would be something much worse than what we saw a couple of years ago during the financial services meltdown.

Believe it or not, the four factors that caused the financial services meltdown exist for the Federal Government's own finances, but nobody is going to bail out America! We have to solve our own problems.

This is where we are headed regarding debt to GDP, and this is optimistic, because this is the latest projection from the CBO (Congressional Budget Office) that assumes we are going to get a lot of savings with regard to the latest healthcare bill. Those savings are unlikely since the Medicare Chief Actuary gave an adverse opinion on the latest trustees' report for Medicare. That is unprecedented.

And what about self-reliance? At the end of World War II, we had the highest debt to GDP in our history, but we had no foreign debt. Americans saved, Americans invested in their future, Americans invested in their country's future, but unfortunately, such is not the case today.

We have, therefore, had to become reliant on foreigners for two things: oil and capital. We are reliant upon oil, and we are reliant upon foreign lenders to finance our escalating deficits and debt. That is not in our long-term economic, foreign policy, national security, or domestic tranquility interest. It is also imprudent. Don't forget: You must pay attention to your foreign lenders. They have more leverage on you; you have less leverage on them. They have already flexed their muscles.

One of the reasons that all of us now guarantee over $5 trillion in Fannie Mae and Freddie Mac debt is because Japan and China demanded it. They had significant holdings in those securities. They were not previously backed by the full faith and credit of the United States Government. They got their way, and the taxpayers will pay the price.

Now, what are our foreign lenders doing? They are going short on their investments in U.S. Treasury securities. There is very little purchasing going on of 30-year treasuries. People have also cut back on 10-year treasuries. Why? Because in times of uncertainty, the United States is a safe haven, and therefore, people are willing to buy Treasury securities because of our rule of law, political stability, the fact that we have over 60 percent of the world's global reserve currency, and uncertainties regarding the stock market. As a result, investors are willing to compromise returns in order to preserve their principal. How do you do that? In the short term, it is Treasury securities.

But the real question is what are interest rates going to be over time, under our present path, and the other thing that the credit rating agencies do not even consider is what is the dollar going to be worth over time. That is why it is very understandable that foreign players are going short on the duration of their Treasury portfolios. As a result, we have the shortest average maturity of our debt of any industrialized nation. That means when interest rates go up, after the economy turns around and unemployment goes down, when there is more competition for capital, we will feel it much faster than others will because we have not locked in these low interest rates for the long term.

When I was Comptroller General, we recommended the Treasury Department go to 50-year bonds, and not only did they not go to 50-year bonds, they eliminated the 30-year bond. Now they have brought it back, but it is not a real attractive investment. More and more, people are going into the TIPS (Treasury inflation-protected securities), which in the short term you do not make much on but which is a good hedge against what the future may hold.

And if interest rates end up going up a mere 200 basis points, 2 percent, it will have a dramatic effect on the Federal budget. Health-care costs are eating our lunch. And if you look at the Federal budget, Medicare and Medicaid represent our primary healthcare challenges, but escalating healthcare costs exist throughout government. Social Security is not the big challenge, and it does not face an immediate crisis. It is not the biggest challenge; however, it is the biggest opportunity in the entitlement reform area.

Healthcare grows much faster than inflation, in part due to demographics, and because we have an equivalent of an arms race for medical technology. Our fee-for-service system also results in perverse incentives. As a result of these and other factors, we spend double per capita on healthcare and we get below-average societal results. We spend double per capita on kindergarten through 12 education, and we get below-average results. It is not a lack of money. We are spending too much money. The system is broken. We have to look at incentives, transparency, and accountability changes to make these systems more successful and sustainable. They need to be dramatically reformed in order to get different results.

You cannot get different results by throwing more money at a system that is dysfunctional, inadequate, and unsustainable. Even in the United States, there is tremendous variation between how much procedures cost, even in the Medicare program, because of differences in practice, and that is why we have to go to evidence-based approaches. Almost 30 percent of Medicare's cost is in the last year of life—and a lot of that makes no sense and is not in the patient's interest.

And what about defense? We spend more than the next 14 countries combined on national defense. Now, in fairness, the dollar goes further in some places than others. Some people do not pay what we do for labor. Secondly, some places are more transparent about their costs than others. But the simple truth is, we take on a disproportionate share of the global security burden. We are doing too much, others are not doing enough, and we cannot sustain what we have right now.

And who pays for all of this? Well, most of the revenue comes from payroll taxes and individual income taxes, only 7 percent from corporate taxes. Who pays taxes? At least 42 percent of Americans pay no income tax. Let me restate that: At least 42 percent of Americans pay zero income tax, and a significant percentage of those get rebates through the Earned Income Tax Credit. Why is that a problem? Because every express and enumerated responsibility under the Constitution of the United States is funded either solely or primarily by income taxes. So that means that these individuals get a free ride on the constitutional role of the Federal Government. That is a dangerous disconnect in a democracy.

These individuals pay payroll taxes, and, in fact, most people pay more in payroll taxes than income taxes, but those payroll taxes are not adequate to fund the programs that they are supporting. There are tens of trillions in unfunded obligations for Medicare and Social Security. And yes, corporations get special tax preferences, and they need to be on the table for reconsideration as well.

We have a progressive tax system. When you consider payroll taxes and income taxes, both, all Federal taxes, the top one-half of one percent of Americans earn 15 percent of total income, and they pay 23 percent of total taxes. But depending upon what their source of income is and how creative they are with the tax system, they can have a low effective tax rate.

Now what about state and local governments? We have discussed the numbers for the Federal Government. Our national challenge is worse than our Federal challenge. Under current policies, state and local deficits are projected to more than double as a percentage of GDP, even after the economy recovers. We are all in the same boat, and bad news flows downhill. We have greater interconnectivity and interdependency along with a number of common challenges that we have to face together.

And what about savings? Our personal savings rate has declined considerably since World War II, and our net national savings rate was negative in 2009 for the first time since the Great Depression.

What are the drivers of government deficits at all levels? They include the factors we have described: expansion of government, health-care costs, retirement income costs, disability and welfare systems, critical infrastructure, education costs, outdated and inadequate revenue systems, and myopia, tunnel vision, special interests, and self interest. And what are some of the things we need to do at a high level? First, when you are in a hole, what is the first rule? Stop digging. One of the first things that we have to do is reimpose tough statutory budget controls that address discretionary and mandatory spending as well as tax preferences in order to stabilize our debt/GDP at a reasonable level.

Secondly, we need to reimpose tough but reliable discretionary spending caps. We need to impose mandatory reconsideration triggers for spending and tax preferences that would take effect when unemployment hits 8 percent. We should not undercut the recovery, but we have to recognize the reality. When you look at leading indicators, structural unemployment is probably going to be about 2 percent higher than it has been historically. We have been eating our seed corn for too long, and we are going to pay a price for it. Long-term economic growth is probably going to be about 1 percent less than it has been because we have been living on the past rather than investing to create a better future.

We should reform Social Security to make it solvent, sustainable, secure, and more savings oriented. Why? It represents our biggest opportunity to exceed the expectations of all generations of Americans. We can show our foreign lenders we can do something and be able to gain some credibility with the American people by demonstrating that Congress can actually get something done.

We need to look at our healthcare costs. As a result of the latest legislation, healthcare is going to increase as a percentage of GDP: You cannot reduce costs by expanding coverage. It is an oxymoron. You have to make tough choices.

Believe it or not, we are the only major industrialized nation that does not have a budget for healthcare. We have a fee-for-service system, which is part of the problem. We have a proliferation of technology. We do not have evidence-based standards. We have not reformed our malpractice system. We have subsidized very lucrative healthcare plans for the well off, and we provide taxpayer subsidies for billionaires who voluntarily sign up for Medicare Part B and Part D. Those are just a few of the things that we are going to have to take a look at, among many others.

We should have universal coverage, but we have to have an honest discussion and debate with the American people about what level of universal coverage is appropriate, affordable, and sustainable. I would respectfully suggest that that is coverage that supports preventative medicine and wellness programs and provides protection against catastrophic accidents and illness for the entire population while providing more protection for the poor and disabled. We can afford and sustain that. The government has promised way too much more in healthcare than they can deliver, including for defense and veterans. There is no way that the current system is sustainable.

We need to do comprehensive tax reform to make our system more competitive, streamlined, simplified, and equitable while generating enough money to pay our bills and deliver on the promises we intend to keep.

We need to reprioritize and reengineer the base of government to make it future focused and results oriented, including the Defense Department.

There is unbelievable waste in many parts of government including defense. The problem is there is no line item that says *waste*, and when I was at GAO, nobody had even defined waste. Waste is taxpayers as a whole not receiving reasonable value for money, both today and over time.

Waste is different than fraud. Waste is different than abuse and mismanagement. Fraud exists, especially in healthcare because that is where the money is, but waste is the biggest problem. Unfortunately, you cannot get to it because it is not as transparent. There are a lot of vested interests. Frankly, Congress pushes a lot of the waste by forcing the Defense Department to buy things that it does not want and we do not need.

And so we have to have some special processes to be able to re-baseline government to make it more future focused and more results oriented. We have a National Commission on Fiscal Responsibility and Reform that is going to report by December 1. We need a new Hoover II Commission that will start focusing on the government to re-baseline and re-engineer it. We need to focus on the future and to generate more results in an affordable and sustainable manner.

A lot of people are talking about doing a lot of things with regard to the defense budget and a lot of cuts will happen because we are in a $62 trillion hole, and that hole grows by several trillion dollars a year by doing nothing, and defense is about 20 percent of the Federal budget and about 50 percent of discretionary spending.

The government has grown too large, promised too much, not delivered enough, and has waited too long to deal with these problems. As a result, we are going to have to renegotiate the social insurance contract, while providing a sound, secure, and sustainable social safety net. We are going to have to re-engineer and reprioritize and re-baseline government, including cutting discretionary spending and constraining it over time. We are also going to have to re-engineer our tax system and raise more revenue.

Our fiscal challenge is primarily a spending problem, but taxes will have to go up. And they will go up on a lot more people than those making $200,000 or more. Why? There is a new four-letter word in Washington, and it is not "debt." No, it is "math." The numbers just do not work. You have people on the far right who say, "We will grow our way out." It would take double-digit, real GDP growth for decades to grow your way out. It has not happened; it will not happen.

You have people who say, "We can inflate our way out." You cannot inflate your way out because while inflation will reduce the burden of the current debt, the problem is not the current debt; it is the tens of trillions in unfunded obligations that will be future debt that grows faster than inflation and faster than the economy grows.

You have the liberals who say, "Well, we can tax our way out." You would have to double Federal taxes by 2035. The American people will never allow themselves to be taxed at that level. We are going to have to do a number of tough things, and we need to do them sooner rather than later, because the miracle of compounding is working against us. When you are a debtor and you delay tough decisions, the miracle of compounding works against you. When you are an investor and you make tough decisions sooner rather than later, the miracle of compounding works for you.

We must make sure that we have adequate resources to protect this nation and to ensure our national security broadly defined, but it needs to be based upon credible threats for both today and tomorrow. We need to do it with the resource constraints that we think we have and are going to have over time.

It is time that we wake up, recognize reality, start making some tough choices in order to make sure that we stay a superpower and that we make sure that our future is better than our past, and that we discharge our stewardship responsibilities to our children and grandchildren.

The Roman Empire fell after a thousand years for a lot of reasons. I will mention four. See if they sound familiar: a decline in moral values and political civility at home, overconfidence and overextension around the world, fiscal irresponsibility by the central government, and inability to control its borders. We need to wake up, recognize reality, learn from history, and start looking at future indicators and comparing ourselves to our competitors and comparators. And yes, we can make these tough choices and make sure that America stays great and the American Dream stays alive. We cannot do it until we recognize that we are addicted to debt, we are addicted to conspicuous consumption. We need to change our ways before it's too late.

We need the 12-step plan for re-engineering the Federal Government, because we have dependencies, and until you recognize that you have a problem, you are not going to solve the problem. And what is going to have to happen to solve the problem is, the first three words of the Constitution have to come alive: *We the People.*

I will do my part. All that I ask is that you do yours.

Chapter Two

Toward a Premise for Grand Strategy

John F. Morton

At the close of the nineteenth century, Britain's leaders shared a belief in the importance of "national economic power," but they lacked agreement on exactly what that concept meant or how it should be measured.
—Aaron L. Friedberg[1]

[T]he successful powers will be those who have the greatest industrial base
. . . those people who have the industrial power and the power of invention and of science.
—Leopold Amery[2]

The greatest danger to American security comes from the national debt.
—Admiral Michael Mullen[3]

In 1945, the United States became the guarantor of an international political and economic system that, by the end of the Cold War, was global. Today, America sustains that position primarily through two elements of its national power: its peerless military and its dollar currency, upon which the international monetary and economic system is largely based. A third element initially enabled that hegemony in the 1940s: the national economy—that is, the Nation's industrial might. Much of that element is no longer present today.

American Hegemony and Its Dependence on a Techno-industrial Base

Academics debate the idea that America's hegemonic role has been roughly analogous to that of Great Britain in the 19th and early 20th centuries, made possible by its Royal Navy and pound sterling. The parallels are striking. Yet often overlooked in the colloquy is an important distinction. Whereas Britain was an imperial hegemon *before* it was an industrial power, U.S. military and monetary hegemony in the American Century was *based* on its industrial power. British institutions for governance—feudal, monarchical, and commercial—long preceded industrialization. In America—initially an agrarian and commercial republic—industrialization preceded its global role and establishment of the present U.S. system of national security governance, institutionalized by the National Security Act of 1947. We are thus left with the question: Does America have the institutions of governance to manage the strategic environment of its apparently "post-industrial" 21st century?

The postwar establishment of the U.S. national security system reflected three strategic preconditions specific *only* to that time:

- America's singular and expansive industrial preeminence, which was undamaged by war, and the means through which it was able to apply transformational technological advances for military use (for example, atomic science) effectively enabled the Allies to win World War II and, under U.S. leadership, reconstruct a postwar international economy.

- At the same time, America and its postwar allies immediately had to focus on a geostrategic threat from an ideologically driven Soviet Union. Moreover, by the 1950s, this single geostrategic adversary had the nuclear weapons capability to threaten the survivability of the American homeland— effectively capturing the national mind.

- Fortunately, though, mid–20th-century America was a time and place when and where a community of interest had arrived at the apex of national power in the political, economic, social, and cultural spheres. Notwithstanding the manifest tensions of the century, this established community of interest at bottom shared a common history and as such was able to sustain a workable cohesion and continuity at the top in New York and Washington, where strategic consensus was generally expressed with the term "bipartisanship."

Today, however, all three of these strategic preconditions are absent. No longer a nation in surplus with an unrivaled, expansionist, techno-industrial economic base, America is in debt and arguably becoming post-industrialized—or, as some would have it, de-industrialized. No longer faced with a single geostrategic adversary, U.S. national security governance attempts to manage strategic challenges that neither generate consensus on prioritization nor lend themselves to military solutions. Yet diverse events and situations like 9/11, Hurricane Katrina, the ongoing debt crisis, uncontrollable immigration, and the BP oil spill in the Gulf of Mexico evince the new and more complex, multidimensional strategic vulnerability of America's heartland "core." Lastly, no longer a nation with an established community of interest providing cohesive leadership across all spheres of national discourse, America is becoming an unbounded space with multiple communities of interest. Most seriously, these communities often reflect conflicting borders-in and borders-out priorities and possess the means to effect them—through favored executive branch departments and agencies[4] and congressional committees with budgetary oversight.

Unfortunately, today's strategic environment frustrates and often daunts attempts to conceive a national economic strategy as a dimension of national security. And like the British at the turn of the last century, we may recognize the concept of national economic power, but we do not agree on what that concept means.

From the beginning of its history, America has pursued to varying degrees three objectives within a national economic strategy, often simultaneously. From 1789 to the present, expansion of national economic power has been a consistent goal. From roughly 1902 to 1992, economic strategy included preparedness or mobilization for war, whereby its Cold War application translated to government acquisition policies characterized as serving deterrence. During the post–Cold War 1990s, emphasis shifted to economic competitiveness, albeit in a form that did not benefit all economic sectors equally. Finally, since 9/11 and Katrina, still-amorphous notions of sustainability and resilience are taking root that may or may not be fully consistent with expansion. War has provided the bookends for each period of evolution, leaving the Nation in a different state than it was before. The American Revolution, Civil War, World Wars I and II, and Cold War mark those passages very clearly. Added to those familiar bookends is the conflated impact of 9/11 and Katrina, which, in terms of evidencing the need to transform American governance, rises to the level of war.

What follows proposes to characterize the evolution of the U.S. techno-industrial base and its relationship to finance, governance, and globalization in an effort to inform development of a national economic strategy for the 21st century that addresses the security and welfare of— to adapt the concept of the British geographer Halford Mackinder—the American heartland core.

From Colonies to Continental Colonizers

As for the familiar conceit comparing the hegemonic role of the United States in the 20th century to Britain's in the 19th, another distinction relates to so-called establishments. Great Britain is a constitutional monarchy, the foundations of which remain on feudal soil to this day.[5] Its commercial expansion was driven by royal charter; notable examples include the British East India Company (1600), Hudson's Bay Company (1670), the Peninsular and Oriental Steam Navigation Company (1837), and Cecil Rhodes's British South Africa Company (1889). British expansion also came through charter, proprietary, and royal colonies. In North America, the New England colonies were mostly charter colonies, although Massachusetts had a unique transition from a charter with proprietary aspects to a royal colony. Mid-Atlantic and southeastern colonies were proprietary colonies under a governor functioning as commercial enterprises under the authority of the crown and answerable to shareholders.

Overall, the British expansionist strategy was mercantilist, predating and generally continuing through industrialization. British institutions of governance provided for and were a reflection of establishment—an aristocratic continuity during these centuries of expansion. By contrast, the United States as a representative democracy pursued expansion in a manner that was led by the private sector and supported by government policies. Establishment continuity was thus not so obvious in America. With respect to an expansionist strategy, it is thus helpful to ask, *Cui bono*? Which regions, economic sectors, and interests benefited?

Seen from a historical distance, following revolution and independence, the 13 original states made a transition from colonies to, in effect, continental "colonizers." The most durable through-line is apparent for the New England states, where surplus agricultural production generated wealth, and a network of rivers provided access to commercial ports and upstream power to run textile mills. Here was the Nation's first integrated industrial and financial base built around Boston to enable an American establishment to pursue expansionist economic strategy. State and local governments raised capital and issued bonds to finance transportation systems—turnpike roads and canals. While not all canal projects were successful, the New England cotton-textile industry saw in them the opportunity to "export" to the rest of the United States. Rapid growth occurred following the War of 1812 to the

1850s. New York's underwriting of the Erie Canal dramatically changed the dynamics. Completed in 1825, the waterway opened the Great Lakes and Upper Midwest to immigration and farming and furthered New York City as a preeminent port, giving it the edge over Boston as the nation's commercial and financial hub.[6]

With advances in steam locomotion technology, railroad construction soon followed throughout New England and the Northeast. In particular, Pennsylvania was able to leverage its own integrated base. The Lehigh River Valley linked anthracite coal and iron mining with an established infrastructure of blast furnaces and incipient manufacturing to generate an extensive regional rail system, all feeding the regional port and financial center, Philadelphia.

In the 1860s, President Abraham Lincoln, whose political fortunes in Illinois were very much tied to rail interests, threw his weight behind Federal support to railroad companies when he signed the first Pacific Railway bill. Between 1850 and 1870, 80 railroad companies received land grants for over 129 million acres, mostly west of the Mississippi River—representing territory totaling approximately 7 percent of the continental United States. This expansionist strategy should be seen as continuing to benefit the industrial-financial interests of the Northeast and Pennsylvania that were vying in the mid-19th century with the slaveholding interests of the South and their pursuit of an agriculture-based expansionist strategy.[7] The Federal Government saw its role as organizing the Nation to develop unified commercial markets.[8] After the Civil War, Federal policy favored manufacturers and railroads over farmers through tariffs and those railroad land grants, which over time would yield recipients huge profits.

These Northern financial-industrial interests thus benefitted and deepened the linkage with Midwestern agricultural processing and extractive industries, which began to change the tenor of those heretofore self-sufficient frontier economies. Another through-line emerged as the Midwest "colonies" began to rebel. At the turn of the last century, the movement was called populism. Later, it was Progressivism. Following the Great War, it morphed into isolationism. By the end of the Cold War, the term economic nationalism came to the fore.

At the end of the 19th century, the United States was on its way to achieving a continental, unified commercial market with a concentrated financial-industrial establishment centered in New York City, the crown jewel of the Empire State. Yet profound social and economic tensions required resolution via a new paradigm of governance. In the years surrounding the Great War, U.S. Presidential leadership embraced a now forgotten concept, called associationalism,[9] first introduced to America by Alexis de Tocqueville. Associationalist leaders—Theodore Roosevelt, Woodrow Wilson, and Herbert Hoover[10]—came from the ranks of Progressivism. Yet associationalist precepts, such as central planning and collective bargaining, came to define 20th-century American governance characterized as the collusion of big business, big labor, and big government.

Many commentators point to Franklin Roosevelt and the arrival of the New Deal as the moment when the Federal Government and the executive branch agglomerated the centralized power through which it governs today. However, this process actually began during Theodore Roosevelt's trust-busting and the run-up to the First World War. Indeed, it continued through the Great Depression and World War II into the 1960s, with Lyndon Johnson's Great Society programs that created large Federal bureaucracies to administer entitlements directly to individual citizens. Nevertheless, the most profound enablers of all that followed dated from the Progressive era. They were the 1913 establishment of the Federal Reserve System and institution of the Federal income tax.

From independence until the Civil War, comparatively modest Federal revenues had come from excise taxes, tariffs, customs duties, and the sale of public land. During the Civil War, the Federal Government instituted an income tax to cover the costs of war. It remained in effect until 1872.[11] After the Civil War, revenues came from taxes on liquor and tobacco, excise taxes, and high tariffs. With Woodrow Wilson's institution of the Federal income tax, the Federal Government had real clout for the first time in U.S. history by virtue of what tax revenues could mean for the size of its budget. The numbers make the point. Justified by war and largely funded by increased tax rates put into law by the 1916 Revenue Act, the Federal budget of 1917 amounted to a sum *almost equal to the total of all budgets from 1791 to 1916.*

Steel as the Foundation of the Early 20th-century U.S. Industrial Base

By many accounts, the Federal mechanisms created during World War II and the National Security Act of 1947, fueled by the 1950

National Security Council Report 68 (NSC–68), gave birth to the military-industrial complex. These ascriptions obscure a deeper understanding of its location in history and how today the classically conceived military-industrial base is no longer central to U.S. economic and national security.

The military-industrial complex evolved with accelerating industrialization in the late 19th century. The genesis can be said to have been during the Civil War, seeded by the railroad interests that had strong representation in Lincoln's war cabinet. Railroads provided the North with a war-winning logistical support capability. After the war, the Bethlehem Iron Company introduced the Bessemer process for converting iron to steel in 1873, followed by Andrew Carnegie's steel-making start-up in 1875 at the Edgar Thompson Works.[12] Through these developments, rail made the transition from iron to steel.

Cheap steel rails substituted for those of iron, creating a continental market for this new technology, which in turn propelled further railway expansion. From railroads, steel made its way into modern boilers, ships, machine tools, heavy chemical manufacture, and bridge and urban construction. Inevitably, the ascent of steel would have military implications—especially for the Navy.

While the rise of American steelmaking in the 1880s was principally tied to the production of rails, the Navy started courting steelmakers. The military case was made by prominent navalists like Captain Alfred Thayer Mahan and Rear Admiral Stephen B. Luce. The first ships of what came to be known as the "steel Navy" were the so-called ABCD cruisers—the cruisers *Atlanta*, *Boston*, and *Chicago* and the dispatch boat *Dolphin*.[13] The first to launch was *Dolphin* in 1884, making her the U.S. Navy's first steel hull. The Navy would prove to be a reliable partner during depressions. For its part, Bethlehem Steel was by 1886 experiencing a poor market in rails and thus looking to diversify. The alliance between steel and the Navy was first embraced by the Democrats and Grover Cleveland in his first Presidency in the mid-1880s. Although Andrew Carnegie was morally against using steel for destructive purposes, his firm did business with the Navy anyway. When the Panic of 1893 depressed the rail and structural steel markets during Cleveland's second Presidency, Navy procurement was there in abundance to insure profitability for both Carnegie and Bethlehem Steel.

Steel also transformed the world of ordnance and gunnery. In 1883, the congressionally authorized Gun Foundry Board established gun factories for each Service. The Navy got authorization to use the Washington Navy Yard. Known familiarly as the Gun Factory, the yard shifted from anchor fabrication to forging cast gun casings and polished liner tubes, becoming fully operational in 1892. The Army got funding to upgrade Watervliet Arsenal in Troy, New York, which in 1888 began manufacturing and supplying 8-, 10- and 12-inch cannons for the Army's coastal forts.

In the 1890s with the rise of steel, the United States made the transition from a Civil War "'militia' theory of industrial preparedness . . . to an integrated system which was capable of meeting the peacetime demands of an expansionist nation functioning in a hostile international climate." Concludes naval historian Frank Cooling, "The needs of the U.S. Navy—like those of navies abroad—became central for stimulating industrial modernization."[14]

From the time of the Revolution and War of 1812 to the First World War, strategic threats to the Nation were deemed to come by sea. Strategic defense of the United States—purely a military function (involving an army, navy, and various state militias)—primarily relied on fortifications defending the Atlantic ports. At the turn of the last century, the new great power industrial capabilities enabled battleship navies to threaten U.S. national security. In 1900, the U.S. Navy decided that the German fleet was the main threat to the Western Hemisphere. As irrational as it may seem today, Washington had a real fear of battleship bombardment of the East Coast, akin to the Cold War fear of a nuclear exchange, a national paranoia more familiar to contemporary policymakers. As much as battleships were symbols of international power and ultimate instruments of sea control, they were also deterrents to that very threat of bombardment.

With the 1899 annexation of the Philippines, moreover, Atlantic sea control responsibilities extended to the Pacific. U.S. industrial capabilities had also reached the point where America could shift its strategic defense doctrine from a reliance on coastal defense to an offensive sea control doctrine provided by its own battle fleet. Sustaining such a fleet (or eventually fleets) required for the first time major peacetime military expenditures, a mobilized industrial base, and broad public support.

Established in 1900 to address such issues, the Navy's General Board was the Nation's first organization to plan for war in peacetime.[15]

To make the deterrence argument, the Navy League, founded in 1903, hoisted as its motto, "Battleships are cheaper than battles." Proponents of latter-day deterrence would make similar arguments for the comparatively costly Mutual Assured Destruction and its successors, the Strategic Defense Initiative (SDI) and National Missile Defense.

Entering a new century, America was coming to grips with the sense-making of burgeoning technological advance, industrial expansion, and its increasing presence on the world stage. Domestically, consolidation in the banking, steel, railroad, and oil industries was giving rise to antitrust Progressive policies to manage the relationships among big business and what would become 20th-century big labor and big government. In the military realm, the transition to the steel Navy generated attempts to align industrial base planning and U.S. national strategy.[16]

Steel was thus the foundation for the late 19th-century to mid–20th-century industrial base. Initially, it had a mutually reinforcing relationship with railroads for accelerated expansion. The steel Navy was the first evidence of the military component of this complex. (Not yet a "big system" Service, the Army would not become a player in the complex until World War I and the introduction of tanks and airplanes.) The matrix of interests based on steel and its applications for railroads (and later the auto industry) and the Navy, together with oil and finance, characterized what can be called the "industrial" phase of the economic element of national power. Its genesis occurred just after the Civil War and would continue to the end of the Cold War. Its organizational expressions tended toward vertical and horizontal industrial integration and were based on fixed and centralized hierarchies.

Meaningful alignment of industrial base planning and strategy would first materialize with the Preparedness Movement prior to the U.S. entry into World War I. Preparedness came with a new realization that war mobilization had to extend from Government-managed resource allocation and production to Government resourcing of the *technology* base as well—specifically, the new fields of electronics and aviation that did not yet have fully mature commercial applications.

Planning for Wars: The Base Extends to Technology

The 1912 elections came at a time when Progressive antitrust sentiment was strong. The trusts had been busy merging or acquiring corporations. New York financier J.P. Morgan was deemed to be at the center of the trust networks, evidenced in the steel industry, the bedrock of the U.S. industrial base. In 1901, Morgan had bought out Andrew Carnegie and formed U.S. Steel. In the midst of the 1907 banking crisis, he had notoriously engineered U.S. Steel's acquisition of a controlling stake in its rival, the Tennessee Coal, Iron, and Railroad Company. U.S. Steel was now in the crosshairs from both ends of its supply chain. Ore producers wanted competitive buyers; railroad operators wanted cheaper rails.

Voters spurned the Republican variety of Progressivism that espoused centralized government power to counter the trusts. They went with Woodrow Wilson, whose approach appealed to small business and more populist democratic ideals. Wilson believed in a national economic policy to balance big business and competition—something that the trusts sought to eliminate. The Federal Government would police industrial self-rule. Wilson was ready to target steel, particularly U.S. Steel.

The President was also set to reform the perceived plutocratic hegemony of big finance made evident after the banking crisis—the Panic of 1907. Congress had put together a commission to reform the banking system with Rhode Island Republican Senator Nelson Aldrich in the chair. Although Aldrich had Morgan representation on his committee, his work pushed a banking reform that would divorce investment from commercial banking and inform the Federal Reserve Act, which established the Federal Reserve System in 1913.

Despite these apparent successes, the onset of war in Europe interrupted the national discussion of industrialism and Wilson's brand of Progressivism. Arguably, when war came to America, the national economy, despite the financial reforms, reverted to the very aspects of centralized financial and industrial power that had been so objectionable to the Progressives.

Ironically, the Preparedness Movement made this reversion somewhat palatable to the Progressive cause. Prominent in the movement was Theodore Roosevelt, who raised his voice in 1914 during the outrage over the atrocities committed by the German army against Belgian civilians early in the war. Other preparedness leading lights were Elihu Root, who had been Roosevelt's Secretary of War and State; Henry Stimson, who had served as William Howard Taft's Secretary of State; and a number of financial and industrial heavyweights like Morgan, Charles M. Schwab, and Pierre du Pont, not exactly regarded as cohorts of Progressivism.

Roosevelt linked his imperialist sentiments with his Progressivist ideals in an advocacy for what amounted to armor and ordnance production. As the peacetime Navy had demonstrated by translating rapidly advancing battleship technologies to ship characteristic requirements, service life was becoming secondary to projections for the life of technology. The stage was set for annual system procurements for an army in addition to a navy. War preparedness now required an industrial mobilization. Those heretofore isolationist Progressives, like future columnist Walter Lippmann and commentator/publisher Herbert Croly, saw preparedness in terms of its potential to advance the liberal Progressive agenda internationally. Others felt that preparedness would require an income tax that would soak the rich and thus serve the domestic Progressive agenda. They found support in the Wilson administration, notably Lindley Miller Garrison, Secretary of War in the first administration; Franklin Roosevelt, Assistant Navy Secretary; and Colonel Edward House, the President's personal diplomatic advisor during the war.

In an informal way, the war in Europe reestablished the trusts before America's war declaration. J.P. Morgan and Company served as the "money trust" by providing the Allies with loans guaranteed by Wilson. It also represented the British to the materiel suppliers in the Northeast and Midwestern industrial belt eager to export to Britain and France. The armor trust, U.S. Steel and Bethlehem Steel, would enjoy fixed prices, while war-generated profits abroad particularly benefited Bethlehem. DuPont, the "powder trust," would profit on explosives. With nitrates as the most important raw material for explosives and food production, DuPont had been able in 1910 to break the Anglo-German nitrate cartel in Chile and thus dominate the wartime supply.

War in Europe and its worldwide effects thus shuffled the deck and dealt a Democratic President a hand different than he had expected or wanted. Two years before the U.S. entry, German U-boats in the Atlantic had a devastating impact on American maritime commerce and presumed neutrality. While Wilson was trying to keep the country out of the war, the U-boat—not the German battleship fleet—induced the Navy and shipbuilding interests to activate a formal alliance between science and the military to deal with it.

The May 1915 German torpedoing of the passenger liner *Lusitania* with great loss of life finally prompted action. The Navy thereupon invited inventor Thomas Alva Edison to chair the Naval Consulting Board in an effort focusing on submarine detection. Edison picked practical-minded engineers and industrialists for his panel, as opposed to scientists. By example, the board's Industrial Preparedness Committee was chaired by Howard E. Coffin, the vice president of Hudson Motor Car Company, president of the Society of Automotive Engineers, and a renowned standards and specifications proponent.

Earlier in the year, the Naval Appropriations Act had established a National Advisory Committee for Aeronautics (NACA) to undertake, promote, and institutionalize aeronautical research. The creation of NACA along with Edison's effort pushed scientists to form their own group in 1916 with major support from the Carnegie Corporation and Rockefeller Foundation, nonprofit entities that reflected the core of the early 20th-century U.S. industrial base and establishment. Called the National Research Council (NRC), it also undertook extensive research into detection of submarines. To this day, the NRC is housed under the National Academy of Sciences, which dates from 1863, another wartime era.

The establishment of the Naval Consulting Board, NACA, and the NRC represented the first steps in the American march toward modern, government-sponsored research—led by engineers, industrialists, and scientists.

At the behest of his Secretary of the Treasury, William Gibbs McAdoo, Wilson met the legendary Wall Street financier Bernard Baruch in September 1915 to discuss the need for and mechanics of actual industrial mobilization for war. A key fundraiser for Wilson's 1912 Presidential campaign, Baruch came with a solid background in raw materials and railroad financing and reorganization. By the time of the 1916 elections, Wilson had fully embraced Baruch's counsel and would run and win on the preparedness issue. The President was aware that under the national leadership in the private sector, preparedness was already under way. The U.S. Chamber of Commerce had been pushing the idea and had made the president of Jersey Standard, A.C. Bedford, chairman of its Committee on Mobilization.

In August 1916, Congress established the Council of National Defense (CND). Envisaged by Hollis Godfrey, a New York banker who was president of Drexel University, the CND was funded by that year's Army Appropriations Act and would ultimately absorb the Naval Consulting Board. The CND principals were Cabinet level: the Secretaries of War, Navy, Interior, Commerce, Labor, and Agriculture. Several months later, Wilson appointed an Advisory Commission of engineers and professionals to provide links to finance, transportation, merchandizing, industrial science, industry, labor, and medicine and tapped Baruch to serve on the panel. While the commission had little power and some 100 committees, the significant ones were on transportation, raw materials, munitions and manufacturing, and general supplies. Representatives came from associations like the American Iron and Steel Institute. The Steel Committee, for example, was chaired by Judge Elbert H. Gary, a key founder of U.S. Steel and a proponent of an industrial self-policing concept called "new competition."[17]

The U.S. entry into the war brought increased demands for economic and industrial mobilization for total war. Within 4 months, Wilson reconfigured the CND's Advisory Commission into the War Industries Board (WIB). Among other things, the WIB was supposed to establish priorities for raw materials, set production quotas, fix prices, and determine wages and hours. However, it was not until Baruch assumed the chairmanship in March 1918 that the WIB began to exercise real authority. A firm believer in national economic policy to forge a government-industry partnership for war mobilization, Baruch looked ahead to implementation of a construct to position American corporations for global postwar expansion.

This American attempt at public-private industrial mobilization for war was similar to what had already happened in Europe. The great power belligerents were settling into a new kind of war—protracted and total. Input came into general staffs and their quartermasters from corporations and private industrial organizations that functioned on behalf of stockholders as much as the national interest. Before the war, the great powers patronized deliberate or command invention only for their navies. Once at war, they saw that the deliberate invention process had to also apply to development of land forces. Technology and industry offered 20th-century operational solutions for 19th-century armies. Not 2 months into the war at the first battle of the Marne, the French reinforced their lines using some 600 taxis to transport reservists from Paris to the front. The stalemate of trench warfare prompted increased military use of aircraft for artillery spotting. The internal combustion engine thus was accepted as a key warfighting technology with potential applications for new concepts like "land cruisers." Nevertheless, armies still lacked systems expertise. In Britain, the army had to rely on the Bureau of Naval Design for the early development of land cruisers (tanks). It was not until the British Plan 1919 that the Service finally embraced the idea of command invention for tank innovation; by that time, however, the war had ended.

During the war, the Navy Department, having a good systems expertise with the steel Navy, had adjusted to the CND Advisory Commission. The Army, however, did not yet have an equivalent peacetime industrial mobilization planning capability that could lend itself to wartime surge. Thus, it had opposed the commission's effort. As a result, when it sent its troops into battle on the Western Front, they could only fight using French heavy equipment. Once it was clear that modern warfare had become mechanized and an arms race in tanks and planes was under way, the Army embraced the need for industrial planning for war. With war's end, however, the War Industries Board ceased operations. Its role in a wartime command economy was a notion too un-American for peacetime, notwithstanding the stresses of postwar readjustment. The Government did see strategic utility in supporting the aviation industry, however. It did so by having the U.S. Postal Service relieve the Army of its airmail service prior to the end of the war and letting contracts for a civilian-operated airmail service.[18] The program generated demand for airplane production and led to development of commercial passenger services.

In 1922, the War Department founded the Army-Navy Munitions Board (ANMB) for the two Services to coordinate planning and mobilization. The ANMB proved ineffective and rarely met. The Navy, having for decades had its own internal planning (the General Board) and industry liaison processes, ignored the ANMB. Undeterred, the War Department proceeded in 1924 to found the Industrial College primarily for the study of mobilization problems. Army planners had to convince the General Staff that plans had to be based on economic reality. This thrust led to the Industrial Mobilization Plan of 1930.

At the forefront of the Army embrace of planning was the Office of the Assistant Secretary of War's Major Dwight Eisenhower, who from late 1929 spent over 2 years of his career on the planning effort. His mentor was former WIB chairman Bernard Baruch, who had been instrumental in getting the office to establish the Industrial College. Eisenhower's work on the so-called M-Day Plan brought him to the attention of Major General Douglas MacArthur, the Army Chief of Staff, thus making his career. In a June 1930 *Army Ordnance* article written by

Baruch's "apt pupil" but bylined by his boss, Assistant Secretary Patrick J. Hurley, "Eisenhower explained that modern war was a conflict between economies; production of the weapons and supplies of war was as important as sound strategy and tactics."[19]

The M-Day Plan of 1930 was the first of four Army interwar industrial mobilization plans. The Service department and Service were not initially in sync, however. In the view of the Army General Staff, supply had to adjust to strategy, and the staff's subsequent Mobilization Plan of 1933 reflected this logic. The Office of the Assistant Secretary of War and the bureaus viewed the relationship in reverse. The later Protective Mobilization Plans of 1936 and 1939 thus adjusted strategy to align with the Nation's industrial potential, reflecting the verities that Eisenhower expressed in his *Army Ordnance* article and that would inform his approach both as a wartime military leader and Cold War President.

Entangled Expansionism: A Nation Not Ready

The Great War had drawn the United States into European entanglements and fueled an expansionism no longer bounded by America's continental coasts and two great oceans. Once entangled, the Nation would require a grand strategy.

As war clouds darkened in the last week of July 1914, British and French investors started to liquidate their U.S. holdings and convert dollars into gold in order for their countries to finance war. The move threatened a run on U.S. gold reserves and financial panic. The financial establishment was not prepared to go through a repeat of 1907—particularly just as the preventive measure to such panics, the Federal Reserve System, was being put in place. By his own account, Wilson's son-in-law, Treasury Secretary McAdoo, at the behest of the governors of the New York Stock Exchange, supported the exchange's 4-month closure to stop the trading of dollar-denominated securities, thus preventing further liquidations.[20]

The U.S. action forced European treasuries to exhaust their foreign exchange holdings, currency, and gold reserves to fund the spiraling carnage. Some countries issued instruments for sovereign bonded indebtedness to allow them to purchase war materiel from the United States and elsewhere. In 1914, the U.S. debt had been $3 billion, primarily to British creditors. By 1917, the Nation would be a net creditor of roughly the same amount by virtue of underwriting $6 billion in war credits provided to the Allies. First evidence of the shift came suddenly in January 1915: as a consequence of the suspended trading on the stock exchange, gold was shipping from Europe to New York in ever-increasing amounts.

"American capital, by itself, could not buy the credibility needed to challenge sterling as international money—only the gold standard could."[21] By wedding America to gold, New York was able to rise above other principally European gold standard centers to become the postwar rival to London.

When the Great War finally ended, the European powers were prostrate. The Continent was in chaos—if not revolution. The Allies would present the Germans with a burdensome bill for $32 billion in reparations. Britain, France, Italy, and other countries owed the United States some $9.5 billion for their wartime loans. The British costs of war required them to liquidate their overseas investments. With the United States emerging from war as a creditor nation, American finance was primed to step into the breach. The Nation was now in a position to complete the shift of international finance from London to New York.

When Wall Street initially had made overseas private investments, they tended to be hemispheric—in Canada and Latin America. American financiers now recognized an expansive potential to capitalize on the opportunities presented by European reconstruction. Loans to help resolve German war reparations could create markets for U.S. corporations, enabling them to pursue export-led growth. Wall Street representatives to international negotiating teams could help establish forward-leaning Anglo-American bilateral regimes (for example, governing oil) and refashion the international monetary system, which heretofore had been dominated by Britain.

Domestically, the war had accelerated change in America. While Europe was in ruin, this nation was bursting with potential. Gross national product had doubled. The population had migrated from the farms to the cities—the United States was now over half urban. Industrialization had advanced. In the rural areas, the introduction of farm tractors generated a shift from family farms to agribusinesses. Developed in the late 19th century for the sewing machine and typewriter industries and then applied by Henry Ford to automobiles, the U.S. mass production capability was without peer in Europe. America could look to a robust postwar world economy, confident that it had the organization, credit, raw materials, ships, and industrial base to restore economic stability and employment on both sides of the Atlantic.

The war had also revealed within that base an emergent community of scientific and capital-intensive industries closely aligned with Wall Street and poised for postwar growth. It was now possible to speak of a techno-industrial base of large-scale firms—in chemicals, radio, and electronics. In 1922, these interests organized around the Institute of Economics, which later became the Brookings Institution, named for Robert S. Brookings, who had served on the War Industries Board. Similar private sector–led efforts had resulted in establishment of such entities as the American Petroleum Institute in 1919 and the Council on Foreign Relations in 1921. The United States was preparing to take its associationalist ideas abroad.

This expansionist drive did, however, expose a fault line in the U.S. political economy. Postwar "readjustment" was stressing civil societies, even in America; in the years 1920–1921, the United States experienced inflation, strikes, and depression. The populist movement railed against the New York bankers, particularly those associated with J.P. Morgan and Company, for entangling the Nation with the European Allies as the result of their wartime loans. Representing a more traditionally minded community of interest were the non–petroleum extractive industries and their small business allies, which remained primarily geared to the domestic economy. This community was isolationist. The immediate postwar Washington policy debate was over American participation in Woodrow Wilson's League of Nations. Lawmakers divided into hostile camps of isolationists versus internationalists— that is, those who identified with the apparent beneficiaries of war.

The league had been a U.S. war aim. It became so through a deliberative process that began several months after America entered the war when Wilson ordered Colonel Edward House, his informal national security advisor, to assemble and chair a group of leading academics to study war aims and peace plans. The hundred-odd group worked from the New York City headquarters of the American Geographical Society. Key participants in "The Inquiry," as it was known, included Isaiah Bowman, the society's president and a geopolitical theorist comparable to Britain's Halford Mackinder, and Walter Lippmann. From their efforts came Wilson's peace plan for the

Versailles Conference, the January 1918 "Fourteen Points." Some two dozen Inquiry members served on the American delegation.

The internationalist voice of Wall Street regarded the German reparations program demanded by the Allies in the Versailles peace treaty as a radical mistake. American financiers deemed Germany central to European reconstruction. Evidence of this assessment was in the work during the 1920s at the Council on Foreign Relations. By far, the preponderance of council studies focused on Germany.[22] With the 1924 Dawes Plan and its follow-on in 1929, the Young Plan—both international attempts to resolve the German defaults on reparations payments—it was representatives from the private and central banks who crafted the international repayment plans that provided for Germans to use a cycle of money originating from U.S. postwar loans to repay reparations. The committee responsible for the latter plan was led by an American, Owen D. Young, president of General Electric, founder and president of the Radio Corporation of America, and coauthor of the predecessor Dawes Plan. Among the Young Plan's provisions was agreement to establish a Bank of International Settlements (BIS) to assume responsibility to collect, administer, and distribute the annuities payable as German reparations. The BIS was a trustee for the Dawes and Young international loans issued to finance reparations. Today, the Basel-based BIS is an intergovernmental organization of central banks that furthers international monetary and financial cooperation and serves as a "bank for central banks."

Unfortunately, the Wall Street crash of 1929 collapsed the repayment system and led to the shattering of world trade. The isolationists in Congress succeeded in passing the harshly protectionist Smoot-Hawley Tariff of 1930. Although President Herbert Hoover opposed the measure, Republicans in Congress successfully pressured him to sign it into law. Protectionist repercussions abroad further deepened the Depression, finally unraveling the international economic system based on the gold standard. In 1931, its 19th-century financial hegemon, Great Britain, chose to devalue the pound and abandon the standard to staunch a run on British gold. Hoover did not follow suit. Foreign investors assumed he would and generated a run on American gold. Instead, he had the Federal Reserve raise interest rates to entice foreigners to leave their dollars in U.S. banks. The following year, in Ottawa, Canada, the British concluded a preferential tariff and trade agreement for the Empire's pound sterling area that reversed Britain's policy of free trade. Germany and Japan responded by erecting their own trade barriers. Franklin Roosevelt came to the Presidency in 1933 vowing to break with Hoover's internationalist-inspired monetary policies. In his First New Deal, he adopted the stance of an economic nationalist and took America off the gold standard.[23] What followed was a breakdown of the international monetary system followed by the rise of imperial or regional blocs.

In the midst of the Great Depression, America turned inward. Internationalism was in retreat. Republican isolationist ire intensified against the forces that appeared to have led to the economic malaise and given rise to the centralized New Deal bureaucratic players characterized as big government, big business, and big labor. The Progressive Republican Senator from North Dakota, Gerald Nye, launched into an investigation of wartime profiteering sponsored by the War Industries Board. The Special Committee on Investigation of the Munitions Industry, or Nye Committee, ran from 1934 to 1935. Among its concerns were the perceptions that the United States had entered into some sort of commercial alliance with Britain and that the pursuit of preparedness had taken America down the road toward a warmak- ing German model of concentrated economic power. The impact of the Nye investigation led to the passage of the four Neutrality Acts of the late 1930s, whose various embargoes only ended with the passage of the Lend-Lease Act of 1941. For the balance of the 1930s, Populist forces and the Depression arrested attempts by Washington and Wall Street to reinstitute internationalist economic policies, even as Roosevelt was shifting in that direction with the so-called Second New Deal. The United States would not reengage with Europe, even in the face of the manifest threat to world peace presented by Nazi Germany.

Instituting Techno-industrial Governance: From War Mobilization to Deterrence

Despite the macro-level anti–New Deal and isolationist criticisms of centralization and centralized planning, interwar mobilization planning nevertheless continued. Accordingly, once war came, military-industrial relations would be better than they were in World War I, except in the minds of left-wing New Dealers, labor, and small business.

In mid-1939, just prior to the outbreak of war in Europe, Roosevelt put Bernard Baruch in charge of creating an advisory War Resources Board (WRB) around his mobilization and planning ideas. Baruch likened the WRB to the CND and felt that it should be put under his authority. Roosevelt was not prepared to go that far and wanted Edward Stettinius, Jr., a Wall Streeter who ran U.S. Steel, to chair the board.[24] While the WRB enjoyed the support of the National Association of Manufacturers and the U.S. Chamber of Commerce, liberal Democrats saw it as a Morgan entity and forced Roosevelt to kill it in November 1939.

After the fall of France in May 1940, Roosevelt resuscitated the CND Advisory Commission. That summer, just after the Republican National Convention, he added Republicans Henry Stimson and Frank Knox to his Cabinet to present a bipartisan, coalition face to his internationalist policies. In turn, Stimson and Knox brought in the New York lawyer Robert P. Patterson, while FDR secured James V. Forrestal, another Baruch associate. Forrestal's effectiveness derived from his Wall Street background. Prior to coming to Washington to serve as the Navy Under Secretary, Forrestal had been president of the investment bank Dillon Read, a Wall Street institution whose networked reach into Washington in the first half of the 20th century was analogous to that of Goldman Sachs today.

A January 1941 executive order formally established the White House Office of Production Management (OPM), which would be led by a director general, General Motors executive William S. Knudsen. Initially, Knudsen was not able to engage the steel and automobile industries, which were not inclined to shift civilian auto production to defense. With the Lend-Lease program for the Allies, things changed. Enacted in March 1941 and initially run by Stettinius, Lend-Lease provided material support primarily to Britain and France and formed the basis, in terms of transatlantic personal and business relationships, of the Bretton Woods Agreements and the Marshall Plan. Defense orders now came to heavy industry. In 1941, three-quarters of all OPM contracts serving the "arsenal of democracy" and Lend-Lease went to the big corporations.

Once America was in the war, the civilian mobilization structure Roosevelt created became confused and convoluted. In an attempt to resolve the confusion, he established in early 1942 another White House mobilization entity, the War Production Board (WPB), led by Sears Roebuck executive Donald Nelson. His efforts were not wholly successful. He was confounded by the military departments. War and Navy had likewise built their own mobilization structures, which proved to be more effective than those of the White House, largely due to their respective Under Secretaries, Patterson and Forrestal.

The White House effort on the research and development (R&D) front was more successful. The threat of war had prompted Roosevelt to consider a concept for a Government-sponsored research entity focused on air defense, called the National Defense Research Committee (NDRC). The idea originated from Vannevar Bush, president of the Carnegie Institution and founder of Raytheon. Roosevelt made Bush the NDRC director with direct access to Presidential funds without congressional oversight. The NDRC work plan was tagged "federalism by contract." Grants went to private research bodies whose researchers would not work for the Federal Government per se but rather would remain with their organizations to form a national research network. The arrangements were similar to those made by the National Advisory Committee for Aeronautics with its network of universities. From June 1940 to April 1941, $3 billion went to the NDRC principals' companies and institutions, something government ethics laws would restrict today.

In developmental terms, as its title stated, the NDRC was a *research council* reporting to the President. It needed firmer legal ground. In May 1941, Bush was able to get Roosevelt to establish the White House Office of Scientific Research and Development (OSRD), which absorbed the NDRC. Subsequent legislation bestowed statutory authority and congressionally appropriated funding. The new name made it a *research and development office*—an organization reporting to the President. As such, it now had authority to prototype small numbers of weapons.

At the highest levels, scientific advances and technological development now fed into policymaking and in turn were themselves fed by massive funding in a command innovation partnership that owed its power to OSRD. Reporting directly to President Roosevelt, its director, Vannevar Bush, was now a czar with almost unlimited budgetary authority. By 1944, OSRD was funding projects to the tune of $3 million per week. Money was going to some 6,000 industrial and university researchers at over 300 labs. In addition to radar and radio-controlled fuzes, the wartime OSRD-backed labs would give the Nation missiles, mass-produced penicillin, and the atomic bomb.

Roosevelt, however, wanted responsibility for the Manhattan Project, the initiative to develop atomic weapons, to go to an organization other than OSRD. He chose to bury it in the Army budget for the Corps of Engineers. Manhattan thus became the Nation's first "black" program. The Army now had another arsenal and armory system that promised to be exponentially greater than small arms and ordnance production. Undoubtedly, the Army bureaucracy would survive postwar demobilization and indeed prosper with a capital-intensive atomic weapon strategy. For the first time, the Service potentially could have a new industrial configuration that would rival the Navy's. If the bomb worked, it was all about the bang. Then would come the question of the delivery system—which weapons platform could best serve to put it on target. Initially, it was deemed to be aircraft; in the end, it would be missiles.

By 1944, it was clear that the military had been organizationally looking ahead to the postwar period. Mobilized defense manufacturing of aircraft and ordnance on a continental scale in the United States had given life to a victorious warfighting strategy. Vannevar Bush did not see a near-term value in missiles and rocketry, but the chief of the Army Air Forces, General Hap Arnold, did, and he took steps to build a separate network of scientific support within his Service. Arnold instituted his own OSRD-type organization in the Army to advise him: the Special Bombardment Group. It was led by the Massachusetts Institute of Technology's (MIT's) Edward Bowles, who was scientific advisor for radar and communications to Arnold and Secretary of War Stimson. "For Bowles, the source of the Army's power would lie in postwar military budgets, likely to reach record levels for peacetime."[25] In the fall of 1944, Arnold, now a five-star general, formed the Scientific Advisory Group chaired by the California Institute of Technology's Theodore von Karman to explore rockets. These efforts by Arnold and Bowles would give birth to RAND, which would become the preeminent think tank for nuclear strategy and deterrence for over three decades.

Washington military planners and policymakers in 1945 were emerging from a global war with hard-won insights. In a purely military sense, they saw that the world had entered an era with a new strategic threat: that of offensive strategic airpower. Meeting it would require a national security paradigm supported by a more formalized peacetime preparedness alliance of government, science, industry, academe, and the military. The environment required new national security structures and processes for planning and resourcing a strategy to maintain a postwar peace and American prosperity. What emerged was a national security establishment that would last through the end of the Cold War.

Once the end of World War II was in sight, the Roosevelt team began to plan for transforming the economy for a return to peacetime. During the war, the driver of the economy was military procurement. The Navy Department under Secretary James Forrestal led the thinking. Forrestal chose a Wall Street colleague from his Dillon Read days, Ferdinand Eberstadt, for this transition task, and for good reason. Even in the early stages of the war, Eberstadt as Army-Navy Munitions Board director had oriented his agency toward the long term—precisely the direction needed to ensure a smooth shift to peacetime production and postwar national policy and organization. Forrestal charged Eberstadt with preparing a report on how to structure that transition.

Thus empowered by Forrestal, Eberstadt assembled a gifted team of Naval Reserve officers and others who had Wall Street backgrounds and Ivy League credentials. Viewing structural problems with a financial lens, he applied Wall Street verities to his designs for solutions.

Eberstadt and Forrestal, as well as Clark Clifford, the Naval aide upon whom President Harry Truman relied for national security insights, saw the world entering a new era with no distinction between war and peace. Eberstadt thus saw atomic-age mobilization as a continuous state, occurring even in peacetime. "Eberstadt's plan would create paths through which business could dominate national security. It recommended formal cooperation between the state and major economic power blocs."[26]

The Eberstadt team presented its report to Forrestal in September 1945. The document became the basis for the National Security Act of 1947, which, among other things, provided for a national security structure resting on three pillars: a National Security Council (NSC), a Central Intelligence Agency (CIA), and a largely forgotten third pillar, a National Security Resources Board (NSRB). "The National Security Council became the keystone of Eberstadt's coordinate system."[27]

His vision was resource-driven. The NSC was to serve as an interagency vehicle to weigh options and advise the President on aligning strategy with the allocation of resources for industrial mobilization coordination. The CIA would provide it with foreign resource assessments for competitive strategies. The NSC would collect its domestic inputs for such strategies from the NSRB, the "basic mechanism to balance the nation's supply of resources with its military demands."[28]

Far from being an unfamiliar idea, the NSRB echoed Eisenhower's conception of an industrial mobilization planning agency as provided by the Army's interwar M-Day Plans.[29] Specifically based on the examples of the World War I–era War Industries Board and the World War II War Production Board, the NSRB was a carryover from the various civilian entities in the White House for wartime mobilization. It reported directly to the President. In policy formulation, it was intended to be the NSC's equal. The NSRB chairman was a civilian appointment requiring Senate approval. Inspired by the influential Bernard Baruch, Eberstadt "considered this agency as the key mechanism to connect [Department of Defense] unification to a larger corporate political-economic organization by coordinating military, industry, labor, and business in a national security program."[30]

Truman and the left-wing New Dealers were suspicious of the NSRB. The President would not go so far as to make it into a War Production Board in line with the intent of its architects, Eberstadt and Baruch. Instead, he wanted it to be merely a body to coordinate mobilization plans across government. In December 1950, 6 months into the Korean War, Truman declared a national emergency and by executive order established the Office of Defense Mobilization (ODM), an independent White House agency that absorbed the responsibilities of the NSRB.

Because of its potential impact on collective bargaining, Korean War mobilization was not fully accepted by labor, whose representatives left various government mobilization boards. In 1952, the crisis over mobilization came to a head in the steel sector, where collective bargaining was failing. Industry hung tough, and labor went into a strike mode, an action that threatened to disrupt the steel supply and cripple the war effort. Truman responded by nationalizing the steel industry in the interests of national security. In late April, he seized the mills. A legal case resulted and quickly went to the Supreme Court. The President ultimately lost in the landmark Youngstown Sheet and Tube Company court decision 2 months later.

The Youngstown decision killed Presidentially led mobilization. Notwithstanding his attempted force majeure in the steel sector, Truman was philosophically uneasy about the NSC and NSRB. He and the New Dealers on his left saw in the NSRB and ODM structures for Wall Street's corporatist managerial elite. Thus, the NSRB never functioned as intended.

Whereas Truman failed to nationalize steel, the United States was far more comfortable in nationalizing the new technology of atomic energy in 1945. Civilians, not the military, controlled the postwar successor to the Manhattan Project, the Atomic Energy Commission (AEC). The AEC management culture was more scientific/academic than corporate—that is, it was without overt and obvious profit and labor concerns. The atomic energy enterprise was gigantic. Some 120,000 employees had worked on the wartime Manhattan Project. The AEC was in effect a government-sponsored monopoly. The cover story of the January 14, 1952, issue of *Time* magazine tells the tale. Titled "The Atom: The Masked Marvel," the article introduced a snapshot of the AEC with the following profile of its commissioners:

> These almost unknown men are responsible for making the weapon that holds in check all-out Communist aggression. They spend billions of public funds, tie up a good part of U.S. scientific and business brains, and operate an industrial empire that may be the pioneer of a new technological era. The AEC controls a land area half again as big as Delaware—and is growing more rapidly than any great U.S. business ever did. Its investment in plant and equipment ($2,174,000,000) makes it bigger than General Motors Corp. At the end of its present expansion program, it will be bigger than U.S. Steel Corp. and General Motors combined. AEC will soon ask for (and probably get) another $6 billion. When this chunk of money is spent on new, strange, secret and dangerous equipment, the AEC will be bigger than the Bell Telephone System, now the largest business organization in the U.S.[31]

Truman's successor, Dwight Eisenhower, finally abolished the NSRB with his national security reorganization in 1953 and transferred its responsibilities to the Pentagon. "[T]his vital corporatist agency [the NSRB] had seemingly been removed from the national security system. In fact, industrial mobilization planning, stockpiling, contracting, and research and development functions shifted to the defense establishment. Assistant defense secretaries and a collection of functional defense agencies replaced the NSRB."[32]

Mobilization may have failed conclusively in the postwar era as something managed by civilians at the Federal level in the White House or an independent agency, but the concept did not go away. Ironically, along with the AEC, it survived under another structure and another name: Pentagon acquisition. The mammoth postwar aerospace and missile programs would thus be housed in the Department of Defense (DOD), effectively a government-sponsored monopsony.

Taken together, it was the mortal urgencies of the Second World War, atomic age, and Cold War that sharpened the concept of a U.S. techno-industrial complex around the postwar conception of a *defense* industrial base.[33] This base supported a perpetual "peacetime" mobilization. Essentially, DOD and the AEC—the forerunner to the Department of Energy—acquisition would ultimately provide the material linkage between the defense industrial base and national security strategy. The size of the Pentagon R&D and procurement budgets relative to those of other departments and agencies was the expression of a U.S. techno-industrial policy—albeit without a name. Throughout the Cold War, Pentagon acquisition would be the government driver for science and technology innovation and a government-created market for aerospace, electronics, and nuclear weapons. In an era of postwar growth, this policy was justified by this market's capability to "spin off" a succession of technologies into the commercial sectors well into the 1970s.

Distinct from the approach taken by the previous Democratic administrations, Eisenhower made no pretense of attempting to manage any peacetime mobilization in the White House. The AEC would continue to administer and fund programs to develop and produce atomic bombs and ultimately nuclear warheads. The Pentagon would exercise responsibility for the means of delivery and the broad range of other complex weapons system programs via defense acquisition.

Upon coming to the Presidency in 1953, Eisenhower initiated the Solarium discussions, which were led by his closest security advisors. Their object was to craft a more affordable national security policy than the national security expenditures supporting Truman's NSC–68, which, along with the costs of the Korean conflict, were busting the Federal budget. The findings of the various Solarium task forces informed a policy to build strong strategic offensive and continental defense capabilities. The resulting policy, outlined in NSC–162/2, was sold as the administration's "New Look." Galvanized by the unexpectedly rapid Soviet advance in atomic weapons, NSC 162/2 recognized that the U.S. nuclear superiority and capability for a retaliatory strike in response to a surprise Soviet strategic attack would not last for long. In a January 1954 speech at the Council on Foreign Relations, as the administration finalized its fiscal year 1955 budget, Secretary of State John Foster Dulles articulated this first real U.S. nuclear strategy, tagging it "massive retaliation." Any Soviet aggression or attack on the United States or its allies would trigger an all-out nuclear attack on the Soviet homeland.

The council, however, received the speech badly.[34] Despite the wisdom of Eisenhower's vaunted "great equation," which sought to balance policies seeking simultaneously to provide security and prosperity, council members regarded the strategy as dangerously restricting policy options. That November, it convened a study group on nuclear weapons and foreign policy led by government attorney Gordon Dean, the former chairman of the AEC. Said Dean with regard to the urgency of such a study, "For all practical purposes we have in terms of nuclear capabilities reached a point which may be called 'parity.'"[35] In the council's view, parity deprived massive retaliation of its credibility.[36] Dean's study director was Harvard's Henry Kissinger. His panel included some heavy hitters in the evolving field of nuclear strategy, notably NSC–68 architect Paul Nitze, Robert Bowie of the State Department's Policy Planning Staff, and Army Lieutenant General James Gavin. Also participating in the study was Republican Presidential hopeful David Rockefeller, who was with Chase Manhattan Bank, representing New York's financial establishment.

In early 1956, the study group reported its findings with an endorsement of gradual employment of force and arguments that would form the basis of limited nuclear war concepts and shape nuclear strategy into the 1960s. This material reached a wider audience via Kissinger's book *Nuclear Weapons and Foreign Policy*, a surprising 1957 bestseller. Among the key findings in the study was the realization that all-out nuclear war demands the use of "forces-in-being"—in other words, industrial mobilization for war in the nuclear age was no longer a viable concept. "The only way we can derive an advantage from our industrial capacity is by utilizing it *before* the outbreak of war."[37] Thus, the transformative impact of nuclear weapons meant that the two geostrategic adversaries would be fighting the Cold War not with their militaries on a battlefield but rather with their techno-industrial bases in a peacetime chess match. "The goal of war can no longer be military victory, strictly speaking, but the attainment of certain specific political conditions which are fully understood by the opponent."[38] In the nuclear era:

> [t]echnical skill and ingenuity were devoted to the design and production of offensive weapons, reducing the opportunities for enemy defenses, but in the process also reducing the demands of professional military talents. . . . The problems of national defense were those of the management of

technical innovation, large-scale engineering projects and far-flung organizations, and of the formulation of a credible doctrine for the employment of the means of unprecedented destruction. The responsible politicians turned to civilian specialists to provide guidance and assistance.[39]

The think tank RAND become "the spiritual, and often actual, home of the new strategy." In a widely read book published in 1960, RAND said, "Essentially we regard *all* military problems as, in one of their aspects, economic problems in the efficient allocation and use of resources."[40]

Engaged Expansionism: A Nation Now Ready

The Dean study group expressed a deeper, irrefutable ground truth. The position of the established community of interest recognized that the Nation was now inextricably internationally entangled, whether the isolationists liked it or not. Nuclear parity meant America could not retrench behind two oceans as it had done after World War I, despite the financial sector's engagement with Europe in the 1920s. In any event, after the loss of China and the Korean War, the isolationists had morphed into unilateral interventionists more inclined to pursue an expansionist policy in the Pacific than to support Wall Street Atlanticism. The debate over nuclear strategy for the remainder of the Cold War would take the form of whether to emphasize pursuit of nuclear superiority or arms control.[41] Eventually, the policy would devolve to what Paul Nitze called "dynamic stability." Both geostrategic contenders in the nuclear arms race, in his view, would come to accept the "lack of need for significant change over time by either side."[42]

As long as postwar growth continued, the community of interest so triumphant in 1956 believed it could apply Eisenhower's "great equation" with guns and butter, both to wage cold war against the Soviets and to reinvent the world in America's image. The Soviets had sunk their money into guns into Eastern Europe and made the costly decision to go nuclear. The U.S. defense industrial economy in the 1950s had the leverage to outspend the Soviet Union on guns to the extent that it would have precious little left for butter at home, much less to apply for policies in the Soviet Bloc or abroad.[43] In the late 1950s, the Soviets nevertheless tried to do so by advancing a series of economic and disarmament initiatives. Eisenhower's trusted propagandist and psychological warfare specialist C.D. Jackson took the stance that U.S.

policy should force the Soviets to spend money on arms to prevent them from releasing it for foreign aid.[44] Jackson's view was informed by a grand strategy that was in the making during World War II and harkened to the Wilsonianism of World War I.

When war once again had come to Europe in September 1939, the Council on Foreign Relations launched what it called the War and Peace Studies Project. This effort performed the same task in the wartime 1940s as did the American Geographical Society's Inquiry for Postwar Planning during World War I. A key player was a major Inquiry participant, Isaiah Bowman. A geostrategic thinker in the Mackinder mold, Bowman, a week after Pearl Harbor, said of America that the "Arsenal of Democracy" "cannot throw the contents of that arsenal away [after the war]. It must accept world responsibility."[45]

In 1940, the project arrived at the conclusion that a German-dominated Europe was more self-sufficient than the Western Hemisphere—unless America could configure another wartime sphere with the British Empire and Far East. The study continued its line of reasoning to argue that the U.S. national interest now necessitated free access to the markets and raw materials in the British Empire, Western Hemisphere, and Far East. In other words, the war required the United States and Britain to move beyond Depression-era protectionism and economic nationalism. The project's aide memoire dated 24 July 1941 on a so-called Grand Area concept proposed a sphere of interest to include the Western Hemisphere, United Kingdom and Common-wealth, Dutch East Indies, China, and Japan. Key was the additional language proposing that lasting integration be achieved by international financial institutions to stabilize currencies and by international bank-ing institutions to invest in development. Essentially, these proposals would create an international system of payments—which was lacking after the interwar abandonment of the gold standard and the disastrous attempt at floating rates that followed. They would build on the Bank of International Settlements established under the 1929 Young Plan, and they would find their way into suggestions made in February 1942 for an International Monetary Fund (IMF) and World Bank. This language was an early enunciation of U.S. postwar strategic goals.[46]

The 1944 Bretton Woods monetary and financial conference in New Hampshire formalized these proposals. Bretton Woods built upon the contractual and personal relationships solidified via the Lend-Lease Agreement. What emerged from the gathering were agreements that established a regulated postwar world economy. In addition to the IMF and World Bank, these accords provided for the Inter-American Development Commission and ultimately the General Agreement on Tariffs and Trade (GATT) upon which to base multilateral trade. For the next several decades, the preponderance of U.S. capital would enable the IMF to oversee the international monetary system. The keystone of Bretton Woods was the agreement that the postwar international monetary system would have fixed exchange rates based on the full convertibility of national currencies into the dollar, pegged at a rate of $35 per ounce of gold, the price set by the 1934 Gold Reserve Act. The dollar would thus serve as the global reserve currency for the world's central banks—in other words, an international monetary system based on the dollar standard.

When America triumphed in World War II, it became a nation with supreme power—military, industrial, and monetary. Informed by the War and Peace Studies discussions, U.S. strategic objectives in the broadest sense were internationalist:

- restore Europe
- establish a world economic and monetary system
- obtain worldwide access to raw materials
- create a favorable climate abroad for U.S. goods, services, and investment
- reduce global tensions.

The war had revealed that the locus of the American industrial base had shifted from extractive industries to manufacturing, as well as toward a structured relationship to government-sponsored R&D for military applications. Extractive combines were now looking overseas for raw materials; agriculture was looking to sell its surpluses abroad. For manufacturers, an economic policy of export-led growth would allow them the freedom to produce by creating a market for their goods. As was the case after World War I, investment banks and capital-intensive firms and their allies in labor and organized agriculture saw in prostrate Europe opportunities for expansion.

The Marshall Plan for European reconstruction met and mutually reinforced foreign and industrial policy objectives, essentially revisiting the frustrated policies of the post–World War I internationalists. The United States would now seed Herbert Hoover's associationalist ideas in Europe and around the world. It would replicate the American managerial and political-economic system to put right the Old World and its empires and keep international order.

Of course, the deepening Cold War interrupted the process. To these strategic goals, the grim acknowledgment that the Soviet Union was already America's postwar geostrategic adversary necessitated another policy objective: containment. The Soviet demonstration of an atomic weapons capability in 1949 and the means to deliver nuclear warheads to the American homeland in the next decade shifted the U.S. strategic priority to national security in what policymakers would characterize as a bipolar world. The paradigm for strategic defense of the homeland and the "West" would remain into the 1980s—even as the world became politically and economically polycentric in the 1960s and 1970s.

Despite the vaunted bipartisanship of the World War II years, this grand strategy had its opponents—generally Midwestern Progressive Republicans, most notably Ohio Senator Robert Taft and Indiana Representative Charles Halleck. Like the interwar isolationists, they were hostile to the Atlanticist bent to U.S. foreign policy. They put priority on the Pacific and Far East, where they saw America as able to function unilaterally. These areas were at the farthest reaches of the crumbling European empires. Along with China, they were potentially the primary suppliers of resources for America. When Mao Tse Tung's Communists came to power in 1949, these opponents of the Atlanticist grand strategy turned from isolationism to unilateral interventionism, believing that— vis-à-vis the Soviet Union—the preservation of American nuclear superiority would enable unilateral interventions. This difference in point of view in the 1940s and 1950s illustrates how those reflecting the community of interest among the extractive industries and attuned to the strategic importance of access to raw materials were not entirely on the same page as those representing another community of interest—the financiers, manufacturers, and traders. Grand strategy during the Eisenhower period required a balancing act for the crafting of his "great equation."

During the early 1950s and into the Eisenhower years, a number of study groups generated papers suggesting directions for the country, akin to what had been done with Woodrow Wilson's World War I Inquiry and the Council on Foreign Relations' World War II–era War and Peace Studies Project. Eisenhower strategist C.D. Jackson put together in late 1954 a high-level conference in Princeton that brought the fruits of these studies together.[47] The Eisenhower-era preference was to promote private investment approaches as an alternative to public development projects characterized by residual New Deal thinking. These efforts by Jackson were to form the basis of America's world economic policy for the balance of the decade and into the next. MIT economists Walt Rostow and Max Millikin collated and published the Princeton findings. Framing them as constituents of a global development project, Rostow and Millikin offered them to the Third World as an alternative to European imperialism and neocolonialism and to the Communist bloc as an alternative to costly struggle with the West. Millikin and Rostow were proposing a threefold approach: a Marshall Plan for Asia, a mutual security program for Latin America, and foreign aid for everywhere.[48] Eisenhower's successor, John F. Kennedy, would eventually modify and pursue these ideas when the Nation began to look beyond Atlanticism in the 1960s.

After the 1961 Berlin and 1962 Cuban missile crises, the United States and the Soviet Union were able to settle many of their geopolitical issues, stabilize the strategic balance, and manage their (by then mutually accepted) spheres of interest.[49] Yet the apparent strait-jacketing of Soviet-American relations fostered discontent in Europe, particularly in West Germany and France, and in China. Both Cold War "poles" of the globe chafed at having to live under an imposed bipolar division. France and China commenced atomic weapons testing in 1960 and 1964, respectively. In 1970, West German Chancellor Willy Brandt pursued rapprochement with the Soviet bloc through his *Ostpolitik*. By that time, the Soviets and Americans were managing—to a degree—their escalating strategic arms race, arguably a costly nuclear parity all along, as they struggled toward and then away from détente.[50] Yet they had been colliding in the Third World for the better part of the 1960s. There, the Soviets had underwritten (with both rhetoric and aid) various proxies in so-called wars of national liberation. The Kennedy administration had responded by exporting the New Frontier via Walt Rostow's widely cited model of economic growth and industrial development as a containment mechanism. The inextricable collision—at least for America—came in Southeast Asia, where the United States committed itself to South Vietnam without a strategy for defeating an enemy and consequently squandered its blood and treasure.

The costs of the Vietnam War escalated during President Lyndon Johnson's watch and led to dramatic increases in U.S. inflation and deficits that stressed the international monetary system. Germany, France, and Japan, whose strong economies had appreciated their currency values against the dollar, held major dollar surpluses. The situation continued to worsen into the administration of Richard Nixon. Fearing these U.S. deficits would reduce the value of their holdings, they had started exchanging dollars for gold. Nixon had the Federal Reserve continue to print money to stabilize the currency. By mid-1971, Germany, Switzerland, and France were opting unilaterally to leave the Bretton Woods system, further accelerating the run on American gold.

In August, Congress recommended devaluation, and Nixon closed the gold window, put in place wage price controls, and introduced an import quota. Critics were quick to accuse him of not consulting with the allies, although governments had already ceased to coordinate their monetary policies. It was clear that the Bretton Woods system would not survive. While the United States was still at the center of the system, Europe and Japan were now credible rival centers of international economic power.

The so-called Nixon shocks of August 1971 further deteriorated relations among the United States, Western Europe, and Japan. The President's New Economic Policy of 1971 unilaterally devalued the dollar, demonetized gold, and raised U.S. tariffs. His critics accused him of returning America to a policy of disastrous isolationism and protectionism. In part, Nixon's economic nationalism was intended to help U.S. exporters and manufacturers, who were competing with foreign imports, as was his introduction of a 10 percent import surcharge that disregarded GATT. But it did not necessarily help the multinational corporate and banking interests.

Nixon's demonetization of the dollar returned the world to the dangerously unstable system of floating exchange rates of the 1930s. Yet the circumstances were significantly different in two respects. First, in the 1930s, the United States may have gone off the gold standard by devaluing the dollar, but it still pegged it to gold at $35 an ounce. In the 1970s, when Nixon cut the dollar loose, it was truly floating. Second, in the 1930s, the international system had fractured into economic and monetary spheres of interests. In the 1970s, however, the dollar was ubiquitous as the world's only international reserve currency. With that realization came another: one country alone could determine the direction of international monetary policy, and that country was the United States.

The Cold War Endgame and the Primacy of Monetary Strategy

Nixon's sharp reversal of American monetary policy, which struck the decisive blow that felled Bretton Woods, prompted a reaction among the internationalists. The theoretical origins to inform that reaction came from Columbia University's Zbigniew Brzezinski. Writing in 1970, Brzezinski said that U.S. policy must shape a new world monetary structure. The United States must further abandon restrictions on American corporations operating foreign subsidiaries and plants in favor of a "truly international structure of production and financing." Finally, policy must reflect a theory of international production to supplement theories of international trade.[51]

Brzezinski was representing the coming of age of so-called transnational or multinational corporations. These private international actors often functioned according to their own interests and priorities—as opposed to national ones. Postwar national policies in Britain and the United States in fact did support such corporations.[52] The American approach, however, differed from the traditional 19th-century British policies. Whereas British imperial policy supported the sending of capital and labor overseas to its colonies and dominions, postwar U.S. policy promoted the dispatching of corporate management to foreign subsidiaries, thereby creating a system where U.S. corporations functioned more like trading companies. While U.S. policy was not imperial, it was not exactly free trade.

As early as 1956, American food giant H.J. Heinz Company received 70 percent of its income from abroad.[53] In the 1970s, foreign subsidiaries produced four times the value of what the United States exported, and most of those exports were internal transfers to those very subsidiaries. As for capital transfers, postwar U.S. policy encouraged corporations to make direct investments abroad. In 1956–1957, direct foreign investments by U.S. firms increased by $4 billion, with 40 percent going to Latin America, mostly in the petroleum sectors, as well as to Africa and the Middle East.[54] U.S. overseas investments flourished—especially in Europe after the 1958 establishment of the European Economic Community (EEC), the original iteration of the European Union. As this trend continued into the 1960s, America became more a foreign investor than an exporter of domestically manufactured goods. In the 1970s, U.S. corporations extended their investments beyond Europe into rapidly developing countries, putting capital in their growth sectors, this time primarily in manufacturing. By 1971, U.S. corporations held 52 percent of worldwide foreign direct investment.

U.S. domestically based manufacturers did not always benefit. In the 1960s, U.S. support for EEC protectionist policies made American exports less competitive. Yet Europeans placed no restrictions on the transfer of U.S. capital into Europe. Nixon reflected these manufacturing equities in choosing to impose import quotas as part of his package to resolve the 1971 monetary crisis. His retrograde economic nationalism did not square with the forward-thinking Brzezinski. The Columbia professor held that economics, science, and technology were propelling nations and societies to functional forms of cooperation with limits on national sovereignty. The role of oil companies helped prove his point. Since the 1920s, the U.S. policy supported use of American oil firms to manage U.S. relations with the Arab world. By the 1970s, once U.S. consumption of overseas oil surpassed the supply from domestic fields, those very firms were increasingly inclined to represent Arab equities.

With support from the Brookings Institution, Brzezinski launched a course on what he called Tripartite Studies at Columbia in December 1971. Brzezinski's work aligned with the views of Chase Manhattan's David Rockefeller. The preeminent New York banker had concluded that financial institutions in America were dominating the industrial sectors of the economy.[55] Further, he proposed to eliminate any restrictions on multinational corporations in their pursuit of world economic development. In July 1972, the banker assembled a 17-person gathering at the Rockefeller estate at Pocantico, New York, to consider in effect a grand strategy with the foremost aim of stabilizing the international monetary system.[56] Among their numbers were former Kissinger associate Fred Bergsten and Henry Owen, both from Brookings, Harvard's Robert Bowie, Ford Foundation President McGeorge Bundy, and Council on Foreign Relations President Bayless Manning. From this Pocantico planning session came the storied Trilateral Commission. The following July, Brzezinski became its director.

The strategic vision that emerged was for streamlining the U.S. economy by emphasizing high-tech, high-productivity, high-profit industries like advanced electronics, aerospace, and energy over labor-intensive, low-tech, poorly competitive industries like textiles and steel. The so-called Trilateralists suffered criticism for failing to appreciate the threat posed by the Soviet Union's determined strategic nuclear modernization. This criticism, however, did not apply to Brzezinski, who as Jimmy Carter's national security advisor pushed for a strong U.S. stance on nuclear modernization and arms control negotiations, which those very critics credited the Reagan administration for pursuing. Ronald Reagan also benefitted from a notably prescient Trilateralist analysis that predicted the declining Soviet economy going critical in the 1980s.[57]

When the Reagan administration came to Washington in 1981, the focus of U.S. national security policy had already returned to the Soviet Union. The United States would fund strategic modernization to counter the Soviet program that had been under way throughout the 1970s despite the jewel of détente, the 1972 Strategic Arms Limitation Treaty. After the Soviet invasion of Afghanistan, the United States was ready to rise to the challenges presented by Soviet activity in the Third World. Reagan agreed with Brzezinski: the Soviet system was going bankrupt. His administration would go for broke with a full-court press to stress Soviet imperial overreach.

At the same time, America and the West had their own stress fractures. Western economies were suffering through what was called stagflation—simultaneous high interest rates and high unemployment. The second set of Organization of the Petroleum Exporting Countries oil price hikes in 1979 had created energy shortages and led to Third World debt defaults. Coincident with the Iranian Revolution, the price increases were leading to renewed moves toward economic nationalism. U.S. economic rivals Germany and Japan were pursuing independent and competitive paths. Although high growth was occurring in information-based industries, the West was facing industrial overcapacity in traditional heavy industry—steel, autos, and shipbuilding—where additional competition was coming from production in the Third World. The linchpin of the international system was still the United States with its strategic power, military alliances, and the dollar. The Carter administration's attempt to manage the system using a multilateral approach was seen to have failed. Ascendant Reagan Republicans and their neoconservative Democratic allies would reassert U.S. unilateralism and supremacy.

Nevertheless, fault lines could be found in the administration. It had fashioned itself with representation from national industries and defense contractors who had formed an uneasy Reagan-inspired coalition with representatives from big banks and corporations more inclined to free trade and détente. The locus of the former was Reagan's circle of White House advisors, plus Secretary of Defense Caspar Weinberger. Representing the internationalist side were Vice President George H.W. Bush, White House Chief of Staff James Baker, and George Shultz, who succeeded Alexander Haig as Secretary of State in the second year of the Reagan presidency.

In the second term, Shultz would emerge as the key player to bring the administration together. Shultz was an economic strategist, a tough-minded moderate attuned to the nuances. His background included high-level work in monetary policy at a critical time: in 1972, just after the Nixon shock, he succeeded John Connally as Nixon's Treasury Secretary. His main task was to pull together a plan to restore the international monetary system, working alongside Federal Reserve Chairman Arthur Burns, Secretary of State William Rogers, Council of Economic Advisors Chairman Herb Stein, Assistant to the President for International Economic Affairs Peter Flanigan, and Under Secretary of the Treasury for International Monetary Affairs Paul Volcker.[58] In March 1973, Shultz assembled the so-called Library Group of finance ministers, which met at the White House. Guided by Volcker's desire for an international solution, this assemblage ultimately formalized into a regular mechanism for international financial consultation under the rubric Group of Six (G–6), now expanded to the Group of 8.

The conservative circle around Reagan emphasized both strategic and conventional defense modernization to further stress the Soviet economy. Reagan's Strategic Defense Initiative (SDI), deemed a wasteful, destabilizing, and technically unsound effort, generated particular criticism at the time. However, SDI reflected the recognition of the deeper truth of the battle of techno-industrial bases that was the Cold War. It was not so much whether SDI could work, but rather with enough resources whether it might lead to a strategic paradigm shift, analogous to that produced by the Manhattan Project. Career intelligence professional Robert Gates offered the best insight: "SDI was a Soviet nightmare come to life. America's industrial base, coupled with American technology, wealth, and managerial skill, all mobilized to build a wholly new and different military capability that might negate the Soviet offensive build-up of a quarter century. A radical new departure by the United States that would require an expensive Soviet response at a time of deep economic crisis."[59] He adds, "I think it was the *idea* of SDI and all it represented that frightened them."[60] In the military realm, in the end, the United States defeated the Soviet Union on the techno-industrial battlefield in a war of budgetary attrition. As Eisenhower strategist C.D. Jackson had foreseen in the 1950s, when it came to guns and butter, the United States was supremely able to out-produce the Soviet Union in both to bankrupt its system and win the Cold War.[61]

At the same time, the Reagan administration had to preserve the Western international system whose multiple fissures posed risks to the American grand strategy. When James Baker became Secretary of the Treasury in the second term, item one on his agenda was the dollar.[62] His approach aligned with the thinking of those behind Shultz, as well as with the international monetary views of Volcker and Brzezinski: preserve the dollar as the world's reserve currency by finding a means for "international economic policy coordination." Baker understood the need for coordination: governments, companies, and investors had difficulty planning for the long term, because since the end of Bretton Woods, it was the market that set currency values. Baker thus worked with other foreign financial leaders to establish a process for multilateral, macroeconomic policy coordination that resulted in the 1985 Plaza Accord. The United States got agreement from Britain, France, West Germany, and Japan to have central banks intervene in the currency markets to revalue the dollar against the Deutschmark and yen. Baker maintained that the accord was a crowning achievement.[63]

Meanwhile, George Shultz emerged unscathed by the Iran-Contra arms-for-hostages scandal that broke in 1986. In the administration shakeout that followed, Reagan gave Shultz the foreign policy lead. The Cold War was already in its endgame. Shultz sent his Deputy Secretary of State, former Goldman Sachs executive John Whitehead, on a fact-finding mission to Eastern Europe. The sojourn revealed cracks in the bloc and in the Soviet Union as well, which, Shultz recognized, prevented the Kremlin from taking action to preserve its control over Eastern Europe. With the Western economies solidifying their macroeconomic coordination on a global scale, Shultz could envision the end. After George H.W. Bush was elected, Soviet Premier Mikhail Gorbachev in a speech before the United Nations General Assembly evinced his acceptance that "the world economy is becoming a single organism."[64] Shultz drew from the remark the realization that Gorbachev was ready to engage with the West and that his desire arose from a position of weakness. The only Soviet strength was in strategic weapons. The incoming Bush administration would arrive with a broken adversary looking for Western economic and technological aid.

And so the Cold War ended during the Bush Presidency with the final economic and political bankruptcy of the Soviet system, stressed by U.S. national strategy. The elements of that strategy only became fully integrated in late 1986 when the Iran-Contra scandal forced the Reagan administration to reorganize. The leadership team that emerged from the wreckage successfully represented and knit together the strategies for nuclear and conventional force modernization with arms control vis-à-vis the Soviet Union, and the various approaches for facilitating international monetary and trade policy coordination with Europe and Japan. In its Cold War victory, the United States thus achieved its broad strategic goals of 1947, albeit almost half a century later.

George H.W. Bush presided over the end of the Cold War and with his national security advisor, Brent Scowcroft, wrote its epitaph: "The Cold War struggle had shaped our assumptions about international and domestic politics, our institutions and processes, our armed forces and military strategy." [65] Observed Robert Gates, "It was a glorious crusade." [66] As for America's future role in the post–Cold War world, Bush and Scowcroft offered their view: the United States was the only power able to "engender predictability and stability in international relations." [67]

The Nineties: (Not) the End of History

In January 1989, the Bush team had assumed the reins of national power with Jim Baker as Secretary of State. The new President trumpeted the appointment, saying, "As secretary of state, he will be my principal foreign policy advisor." [68] As for his foreign policy expertise, Baker claimed his previous international work in the Treasury Department with the world's finance ministers and central bankers. [69] Baker's assessment of his appointment was an early signal of what promised to be a post–Cold War power shift in Washington and the Executive Branch: the decline of the Pentagon and the rise of Treasury and the Federal Reserve. As the Nation proceeded into the 1990s, it would become clear how the strategic priorities, whether expressed in declaratory policy or not, would move from considerations of national security informed by the community of interest around the defense techno-industrial base to those of monetary policy counseled by a community associated with the financial services sector.

Narrowly conceived, the Federal Reserve was supposed to supervise and regulate banks, implement monetary policy, and maintain a strong official payments system. In August 1987, Alan Greenspan had become its chairman. Greenspan took the position that the Federal Reserve should assume a more activist role by adopting policies of market interventions—policies somewhat beyond those of free-market economics. Under Greenspan, Washington thus would have a regulatory policy for the financial services sector (read *bailouts*). Prompted initially by the credit and debt crises of the 1980s, the dollar value of these accelerating interventions would eventually rival the oft-criticized Pentagon budget amounts that benefitted the sometimes maligned Cold War military-industrial complex. As the Cold War priorities began to recede and the impact of the 1980s debt crises began to be felt, political power realigned toward lenders, banks, investment firms, mutual funds, and the like.

The 1990s would prove to be a decade without any sustained global national security distractions. Policymakers could finally and fully address the formalizing of the international monetary and trading regimes envisaged in 1944 at Bretton Woods. Fifty years on, the international political-economic system was markedly different: the new fact of life was globalization.

The United States may have entered the 1990s as the world's sole superpower. Absent a geostrategic military rival, the military component of national strategy quickly assumed diminished importance. Yet initially, the U.S. military-industrial sector and defense policymakers did not recognize the full extent of the meaning of globalization. Abroad was a very competitive Japan and a Europe moving toward some sort of union under what was at the time tagged "EC 92." The American defense community saw potential geostrategic rivals converging into neomercantilist blocs. In response, defense managers proposed to apply "competitive strategies," a concept developed during the Cold War endgame. The approach had relied on net assessments to make the material link between operational concepts, specifically for North Atlantic Treaty Organization warfighting, and acquisition. In the post–Cold War era, advocates sought to translate this approach to strategies for economic competitiveness. They aligned themselves with another carryover initiative to identify, prioritize, leverage, and acquire critical technologies that would serve as a basis for informing a U.S. techno-industrial policy. The model was the late 1980s government-funded 14-member Sematech consortium for semiconductor manufacturing, the U.S. attempt to regain competitiveness in the information technology (IT) base vis-à-vis Japan. Sematech enthusiasts assumed that the vaunted "peace dividend" afforded by the end of the Cold War could reprogram to underwrite similar efforts to retool American manufacturing—for example, by making it agile—for other critical technologies that offered a competitive, high-tech value-add. Sematech, however, was not repeated.

The majority opinion among Republicans and Democrats opposed use of any techno-industrial policy that would "pick winners and losers."

At the same time, facing certain cuts to Pentagon budgets, tier-one prime contractors put emphasis on loosening export control policies. In their pursuit of the anticipated closing of the common European defense market, they secured—when and where they could—approvals for offset agreements, at the expense of their own third-tier defense suppliers in America, to overcome nontariff barriers such as rules of origin and local content requirements. These global strategies led to the point where some tier-two defense electronics firms, notably EDS Defence, were unabashedly claiming to be "stateless corporations."

The consumer electronics sector in the 1980s and 1990s was driving technology advances. Whereas in the Cold War era, the defense sector generated "spinoff" technologies for the commercial sector, the private sector had surged ahead offering "spin-in" technologies for defense applications, notably in IT, the EDS core competency. In short, the defense and the commercial techno-industrial bases had merged and were no longer conceived as a "national" base but rather as enterprise elements exchanging intellectual property, human resources, goods, services, and capital in a global commons.

Advances in information technology enabled corporations to flatten their organizational structures. No longer traditional hierarchies, corporations were moving toward network structures. They were embracing joint ventures and strategic alliances, often with foreign partners. Transnational corporations could use IT to accelerate their use of global R&D and manufacturing strategies. In a move away from fixed assets, which stranded capital, they could outsource and implement just-in-time logistics management strategies whereby they could "warehouse" inventories in the supply chain, a strategy that assumed that strategic-level security threats would remain things of the past and a distant concern.

Corporations made competitive assessments based on an increasing capability to use IT to develop and perfect algorithms for return on investment. In the early 1980s, a trend became evident. Increasing numbers of institutional investors were serving on corporate boards. Accordingly, major corporations began to assess themselves differently, no longer simply looking at production as their profit centers; their financial services divisions suddenly became more interesting. These divisions are now very familiar: examples include General Motors' GMAC and General Electric's GE Capital, both of which are heavily into home mortgages and commercial financing—far removed from what their core businesses were during America's industrial era.

Whatever date or event historians may ascribe as the precise end of the Cold War, Bill Clinton was inaugurated in January 1993 as the first post–Cold War President. In a sense, the 1990s were comparable to the post–World War II era when the United States pursued European reconstruction via the Marshall Plan. In that respect, the Clinton administration would continue its predecessor's policy to resource development in Eastern Europe and the former Soviet republics, adding to it the objective of arriving at some kind of economic and security condominium with China. As for national security, the administration cut Pentagon acquisition, privatized defense functions, and changed the mission of the Department of Energy nuclear complex of laboratories and sites from development and production of nuclear weapons to "environmental management." In effect, the Clinton administration put an end to what had been America's Cold War techno-industrial policy.

In its stead, the administration adopted a policy associated with Third Way centrism. Its adherents in Britain and America proposed to build upon the policies of Prime Minister Margaret Thatcher and President Reagan that embraced deregulation, privatization, and globalization. In effect, the techno-industrial policy that emerged for the 1990s would benefit not defense, but telecommunications, the utilities, and financial services.

In terms of pure size, the financial services sector was America's biggest, outstripping manufacturing, health, wholesale/retail, and agriculture. The community of interest was a constellation around a core of Wall Street investment banking and the Federal Reserve Bank of New York. Yet whereas the investment bankers had served the interests of their shareholders, the profusion of shadow banking mechanisms and instruments made loyalty somewhat situational.

For the most part, shadow banking arose as one consequence of the floating currency exchange rates following the breakdown of Bretton Woods. No longer were governments effectively able to use controls as principal means to administer monetary policy and the supply of money. When the dollar ceased to be based on gold convertibility, it became based on projected future value, and that entailed risks that needed to be hedged. By the 1990s, the widespread use of hedge funds, derivatives, credit default swaps, and other financial instruments to address risk could also serve as vehicles for speculation, spawning the unregulated world of shadow banking. In this world, loyalty was now to the "deal." And more often, the deal was a financial instrument for some aspect of an enterprise in the global commons whose raison d'etre was just that—the deal. The decade was all about the mobility of capital—indeed, though still denominated in dollars, capital that was stateless. In sum, globalization was really the globalization of financial markets.

If Henry Kissinger had the stature of a Metternich of the Cold War, Robert Rubin was the Cavour of the New World Order. As the co-chairman of Goldman Sachs, Rubin participated in Clinton's transition team. By this time, Goldman had become the Dillon Read of the end of the American Century. In 1968, John Whitehead had led the firm toward a global and strategically minded enterprise. Whitehead brought Lyndon Johnson's Treasury Secretary, Henry Fowler, to the firm. At the same time, he turned Goldman into the first international investment banking firm, establishing a London office with the capability to offer American-style commercial paper, corporate promissory notes, in a sense equivalent to government-issued paper currency.

In his 2003 memoir, Rubin says the global priorities were clear to Clinton's transition team. When the President-elect's economic policy advisors considered bond markets, they took as their starting point for analysis and advice the international—as opposed to the U.S.—bond market. Rubin determined that his role as Clinton's Secretary of the Treasury would be to craft policy precisely on the basis of a globalization of financial markets.[70] Other authors cite a September 1993 speech by National Security Advisor Anthony Lake at Johns Hopkins University as the key statement of what was going to be the Clinton administration's grand strategy focus. Lake spoke of the transition from a policy of containment to a policy to enlarge market democracies.[71] In effect, this approach was a continuation of the postwar policies of the two wars, which were interrupted by the Cold War. Rubin and Clinton stood for free trade, financial deregulation, and IMF leverage to further international monetary and economic policy coordination. The United States would serve as the facilitator of a single, globalized market. Its security responsibilities would be to maintain peace and stability to enable multilateral banking and trade to thrive further.

Rubin and his senior Treasury team,[72] which included Larry Summers, Tim Geithner, David Lipton, and Caroline Atkinson, worked closely with Alan Greenspan to craft policies that supported the Federal Reserve chairman's goals for American banking when he succeeded Paul Volcker in 1987. In the last decade of the 20th century, international banking was dominated by superbanks such as the Japanese Mitsubishi, the British Hong Kong Shanghai Banking Corporation (HSBC), the Swiss Credit Suisse, and the German Deutsche Bank. When Greenspan became chairman, the United States had no banks in the world's top ten. Greenspan and the Federal Reserve became advocates of the idea that America should have its own super-banks to compete. Federal Reserve policy thus moved to support the idea. After a decade as chairman, Greenspan was able to say that the Fed was able not only to cut interest rates but also bail out banks—and, like the Bank of Japan, intervene in "market events." It could, for example, buy futures or equities from mutual funds and other institutional sellers to forestall panic and pump money into the system. It could even buy state and local debt, real estate, or gold mines.[73] With a Washington policy for bailouts, the Federal Reserve provides liquidity and benign regulation. In effect, Greenspan's approach was an industrial policy for the U.S. financial services sector. The repeal of the 1933 Glass-Steagall Act in the 1999 Financial Services Modernization Act, which eliminated the barriers to commercial banking, insurance, securities, and mort-gages, was the final enabler for Greenspan's superbanking competitive strategy. By 2003, the United States had three banks in the world's top ten. Citigroup stood at number one, accompanied in the rankings by Bank of America and JPMorgan Chase.

The enhanced confluence of the Federal Reserve and Treasury in the 1990s elevated the monetary policy of the United States to a postwar grand strategy built around the Nation's superbanks as the competitive core and the dollar as *the* U.S. export. The techno-industrial base would appear no longer to be the American core. As always, the numbers tell the tale. In 1950, just into the start of the Cold War, manufacturing represented 29.3 percent of gross domestic product (GDP); finance was a mere 10.9 percent. That year, manufacturing generated over 50 percent of U.S. corporate profits; finance accounted for 10. Fifty-five years later in 2005, manufacturing provided just 12 percent of GDP, while finance contributed 20.4. Yet the really telling numbers are that year's figures on corporate profits: in 2005, manufacturing tallied less than 10 percent, while finance was responsible for 40 to 50 percent of all corporate profits in the United States.

In today's national economic policy debates, the globally oriented financial services sector is dominant over what had been the Cold

War military-industrial complex, many of whose elements are more nationally oriented. The post–Cold War budgetary retrenchment in the 1990s consolidated this complex into a handful of behemoth defense firms, such as Lockheed Martin, Northrop Grumman, Boeing, Raytheon, and General Dynamics. The Pentagon monopsony gave way to these defense-industrial "trusts," reduced to begging for business. If Lockheed Martin represents the first among equals "inside the Beltway," it is Goldman Sachs who is the big dog with Washington suasion on Wall Street. Once, the industrial policy debates had been over "picking winners and losers." In the first decade of the 21st century, the debates are over "too big to fail."

And what geostrategic threat now rises to focus the national mind on a grand strategy? After 9/11, the George W. Bush administration tried to tie rogue states with weapons of mass destruction capabilities to al Qaeda to pursue a global war on terror. Some saw this as, at best, a declaratory policy. They would argue that the Bush grand strategy was a resource strategy, the subject addressed by Vice President Dick Cheney's National Energy Policy task force. Or is it, at bottom, preservation of the dollar as the international reserve currency? If so, the threat could be coming from a truly geostrategic rival who not only holds a significant amount of our national debt but is also developing information warfare capabilities that could end American life as we know it without firing a shot. Can we assume that we can manage this cyberspace standoff as successfully as we did with nuclear deterrence? And swimming in an ocean of debt, how does our nation resource what remains of our heartland (if such a descriptive still has meaning) techno-industrial base to rise to these challenges?

History indeed is without end. We have our work cut out for us.

Notes

[1] Aaron L. Friedberg, *The Weary Titan: Britain and the Experience of Relative Decline, 1895–1905* (Princeton: Princeton University Press, 1988), 79.

[2] Leopold Amery, "Comments on Mackinder," *Geographical Journal* 23 (1904), 439–441.

[3] Admiral Mike Mullen, USN, Chairman of the Joint Chiefs of Staff, August 26, 2010.

[4] Today, most notably the Pentagon, Treasury, and Federal Reserve.

[5] All properties in England and Wales are either freehold or leasehold. The owner of freehold properties fully owns the land and buildings. Leasehold properties do not include ownership of the land and in some cases the buildings—for example, in the case of apartments. Leaseholders are granted the right to live there by the freeholder and own the property for as long as the lease specifies. Many leases were originally granted for up to 999 years, but existing leases on properties

are usually shorter—for example, 99 years. At the end of the lease, possession of the property reverts to the freeholder. The largest freeholders in the West End of London include the Queen, the Church of England, the Duke of Westminster, the Earl of Cadogan, the Howard de Waldens, and Viscount Portman.

[6] The Federal Government also provided support for transportation infrastructure projects. The noteworthy example was the Cumberland or National Road over the Allegheny Mountains. Construction began in 1811 at Cumberland, Maryland, and finished in 1818 in Wheeling, on the Ohio River, in what is now West Virginia. A series of turnpikes connected the road to Baltimore by 1824. To the west, the National Road continued to Illinois, finishing in Vandalia in 1839.

[7] Although the United States sees itself as the historical champion of free trade, New England and the North were generally protectionist at this time, whereas the South was for free trade. At issue was the use of tariffs to protect infant industries—an industrial policy, as it were, that benefitted the North. The Southern and Midwestern agricultural interests, which were at the time generating the vast majority of U.S. exports, did not wish to see America contributing to tariff wars with Europe and European colonies—their overseas markets. Moreover, not having their own regional industrial bases, they did not want the costs of imported manufactures burdened by further costs imposed by high Federal protectionist tariffs. This disconnect was a continuance of the creative tension that began with the Founding Fathers, specifically New York's Alexander Hamilton and Virginia's Thomas Jefferson, and endures as an American historical narrative motif. In the 19th century, tariff policy was one key manifestation that divided centralizing industrial and financial interests from decentralized agrarian and small business interests in the South and Midwest. Then, tariffs were the principal means for the Federal Government to collect revenue. Yet high tariffs protected home industry and further supported those deemed critical to the Nation's defense, an argument put forth by Kentucky Hamiltonian Henry Clay on behalf of his so-called American System, which included policies for Federal funding of infrastructure projects and a strong national bank.

[8] Postwar American policymakers essentially took this approach and applied it to Europe with the Marshall Plan.

[9] Michael J. Hogan, *The Marshall Plan: America, Britain, and the Reconstruction of Western Europe, 1947–1952* (Cambridge: Cambridge University Press, 1987), characterizes the American version of the "associative state" as having a:

> political economy founded on self-governing economic groups, integrated by institutional coordinators and normal market mechanisms, led by cooperating public and private elites, nourished by limited but positive government power, and geared to an economic growth in which all could share. These efforts married the older traditions associated with the localized and fragmented political economy of the nineteenth century, including individualism, privatism, competition, and antitrust, to the twentieth-century trend toward an organized capitalism characterized by national economies of scale, bureaucratic planning, and administrative regulation. (3)

[10] Prior to his political career, Hoover was a mining engineer. His brand of associationalism owed much to Fredrick Winslow Taylor's Efficiency Movement. In Britain prior to the Great War, Halford Mackinder was identified with the British iteration, the National Efficiency Movement. The effort, championed by Mackinder while at the London School of Economics, had similar technocratic goals—for example, to reverse the deterioration of efficiencies in the military, business, and government administration, first revealed in the Boer War, oft cited as Britain's Vietnam.

[11] After the Panic of 1893, President Grover Cleveland restored the income tax until the Supreme Court declared it unconstitutional in 1895.

[12] Carnegie named the works after the Pennsylvania Railroad president, in homage to Thompson's mentoring him as a young man.

[13] The Industrial College of the Armed Forces' Benjamin Franklin Cooling marks these awards as the origin of the Nation's military-industrial complex. See Cooling, *Gray Steel and Blue Water Navy: The Formative Years of America's Military-Industrial Complex 1881–1917* (Hamden, CT: Archon Books, 1979), 55.

[14] Ibid., 12–13.

[15] John S. Craighill, David E. Jeremiah, Howard K. Schue, and John F. Morton, "The Navy General Board: Balance Wheel to Receiving Ship," *Technology Strategies and Alliances*, Report to the Office of Net Assessment, March 31, 2005.

[16] To be sure, a case can even be made that presteel shipbuilding "industrial" base priorities were evident in Federal policies as far back as the early years of the Republic. By example, 3 years into the 19th century, Congress recognized the importance of the shipbuilding base after fire ravaged Portsmouth, New Hampshire. The Congressional Fire Disaster Act of 1803, which provided ad hoc assistance to the city, was the first instance of Federal disaster legislation. At the time, Portsmouth was not only the cradle of American shipbuilding but also a major port whose commerce provided the Federal Government with substantial tariff revenues.

[17] Gary, from whom the city of Gary, Indiana, takes its name, brought together Morgan, Carnegie, and Schwab to create U.S. Steel and served as its president and board chairman.

[18] Similarly, the Federal Government had contracted with steamship companies starting in 1847 and railroad companies in 1869.

[19] Kerry E. Irish, "Apt Pupil: Dwight Eisenhower and the 1930 Mobilization Plan," *Journal of Military History* 70 (January 2006), 40.

[20] William Gibbs McAdoo, *Crowded Years: The Reminiscences of William G. McAdoo* (Port Washington, NY: Kennikat Press, 1931), 290.

[21] William L. Silber, *When Washington Shut Down Wall Street:The Great Financial Crisis of 1914 and the Origins of America's Monetary Supremacy* (Princeton: Princeton University Press, 2007), 168.

[22] Robert D. Schulzinger, *The Wise Men of Foreign Affairs: The History of the Council of Foreign Relations* (New York: Columbia University Press, 1984), 22.

[23] In fact, it was the Gold Reserve Act of 1934 that changed the nominal dollar price of an ounce of gold from $27.67 to $35. The dollar itself was thus pegged; it did not float against gold.

[24] Along with Stettinius, the WRB had Walter S. Gifford of AT&T, Harold G. Moulton, president of Brookings, Karl Compton of MIT, John Lee Pratt of GM, and Robert E. Wood of Sears—but not Baruch.

[25] G. Pascal Zachary, *Endless Frontier: Vannevar Bush, Engineer of the American Century* (New York: The Free Press, 1997), 229.

[26] Jeffrey M. Dorwart, *Eberstadt and Forrestal: A National Security Partnership* (College Station, TX: Texas A&M University Press, 1991), 105.

[27] Ibid., 106.

[28] Ibid.

[29] Irish, 40–41.

[30] Dorwart, 155.

[31] "The Atom: The Masked Marvel," *Time*, January 14, 1952, available at <www.time.com/time/magazine/article/0,9171,806177,00.html#ixzz0fXoL6Tqb>.

[32] Dorwart, 178–179.

[33] Over time, the notion of a defense industrial base assumed a somewhat negative cast as the military-industrial complex, famously enunciated in 1961 by President Eisenhower in his farewell address to the Nation.

[34] Schulzinger, 150.

[35] Gordon Dean, foreword to Henry A. Kissinger, *Nuclear Weapons and Foreign Policy* (New York: Harper & Brothers, 1957), vii.

[36] Paul H. Nitze, *From Hiroshima to Glasnost: At the Center of Decision* (New York: Grove Weidenfeld, 1989), 151–152. Nitze wrote that in the State Department view, massive retaliation reduced the value and effectiveness of diplomacy. He himself saw it as ending the wartime and postwar bipartisan foreign policy consensus. By 1955, it was clear to him that massive retaliation was only a declaratory policy. In actual fact, he wrote, the policy had become graduated deterrence.

[37] Kissinger, 93.

[38] Ibid., 225.

[39] Lawrence Freedman, *The Evolution of Nuclear Strategy,* 2[d] ed. (New York: St. Martin's Press, 1989), 175–176.

[40] Ibid.

[41] Robert Gates has addressed at length a hidden bipartisan continuity to Cold War policy: "Hidden because, regardless of philosophy, the public approach of challengers in our politics is usually to tear down rather than to promise to build upon the work of incumbents—especially if the incumbent is in the other party. . . . Indeed, I believe that the conventional wisdom that Vietnam shattered the American consensus in foreign policy was not borne out by experience." Liberals, he says, opposed CIA operations; conservatives felt its assessments were too soft and supportive of arms control. "The terms 'hawks' and 'doves' do oversimplify the contending factions in the American government from 1969 to 1991." Gates says disputes occurred in all five Presidencies in which he served, but "these disputes were neither unusual nor weakening. They represented, in fact, a healthy contention of ideas and approaches. . . . Presidents needed both hawks and doves, because this aviary mixture allowed the Presidents, more often or not, to be the 'owls.'" Robert M. Gates, *From the Shadows: The Ultimate Insider's Story of Five Presidents and How They Won the Cold War* (New York: Simon & Schuster, 1996), 556–571.

[42] Nitze, 170.

[43] This situation was a geostrategic reversal of Mackinder's axiom, "Who rules East Europe commands the Heartland. Who rules the Heartland commands the World-Island. Who rules the World-Island commands the World."

[44] Blanche Wiesen Cook, *The Declassified Eisenhower: A Divided Legacy* (Garden City, NY: Doubleday and Company, 1981), 325.

[45] Laurence H. Shoup and William Minter in *Trilateralism: The Trilateral Commission and Elite Planning for World Management*, ed. Holly Sklar (Boston: South End Press, 1980), 146.

[46] Ibid., 142.

[47] One study was the November 1950 Gray Report, led by Gordon Gray and Edward S. Mason, which focused on Third World development. Another was the March 1951 Rockefeller Report, recommending a new international finance agency. Others were the June 1952 Paley Report on raw materials, the February 1953 Bell Report on trade and tariff policy, and the January 1954 Randall Report on world shortage of dollars, the so-called "dollar gap." Cook, 304–307.

[48] Ibid., 309.

[49] Jeremi Suri, *Power and Protest: Global Revolution and the Rise of Détente* (Cambridge: Harvard University Press, 2003), 95.

[50] Robert Gates wisely observed:
> Détente's greatest achievement was the opening of consistent contact between the United States and the USSR in the early 1970s—a gradually intensifying engagement on many levels and in many areas that, as it grew over the years, would slowly but widely open the Soviet Union to information, contacts, and ideas from the West and would facilitate an ongoing East-West dialogue that would influence the thinking of many Soviet officials and citizens. At the same time, détente was discredited after 1974 because, by then, it was readily apparent that neither power was prepared to change its basic adversarial approach to the competition. Further, neither party could get from détente what it most wanted. The United States wanted to stop the Soviet arms build-up and to obtain Soviet help in extracting itself from Indochina. It was unsuccessful on both counts. The Soviets wanted an ally against China and help in dealing with its increasingly severe economic problems. It, too, was unsuccessful on both counts.
>
> Gates, 49.

[51] Zbigniew Brzezinski, *Between Two Ages: America's Role in the Technetronic Era* (New York: Viking Press, 1970), 300.

[52] For example, in 1954, U.S. firms were getting tax breaks on profits earned from overseas subsidiaries. Cook, 303.

[53] Ibid., 322.

[54] Ibid., 319.

[55] Peter Collier and David Horowitz, *The Rockefellers: An American Dynasty* (New York: Holt, Rinehart and Winston, 1976), 407.

[56] Sklar, 484.

[57] Ibid., 34.

[58] George P. Shultz, *Turmoil and Triumph: My Years as Secretary of State* (New York: Charles Scribner's Sons, 1993), 147.

[59] Gates, 264.

[60] Ibid., 266.

[61] In their 1957 *Nuclear Weapons and Foreign Policy*, the Dean study group interestingly observed that once the Soviets had nuclear weapons, they suddenly had an ideological problem. A sustained nuclear stalemate compromised the root Marxist doctrine of historical inevitability. Nuclear weapons established that the forces of technology were superior to the forces of history and demonstrated that technological innovations could paralyze the dialectic of class struggle. Kissinger, 384.

[62] James A. Baker III, *"Work Hard, Study . . . and Keep Out of Politics!" Adventures and Lessons from an Unexpected Public Life* (New York: G.P. Putnam's Sons, 2006), 428.

[63] Ibid., 426–432.

[64] Shultz, 1107.

[65] George Bush and Brent Scowcroft, *A World Transformed* (New York: Alfred A. Knopf, 1998), 564.

[66] Gates, 574.

[67] Bush and Scowcroft, 566.

[68] Baker, 283.

[69] Ibid., 282.

[70] Robert E. Rubin, *In an Uncertain World: Tough Choices from Wall Street to Washington* (New York: Random House, 2003), 121.

[71] Derek Chollet and James Goldgeier, *America Between the Wars From 11/9 to 9/11: The Misunderstood Years Between the Fall of the Berlin Wall and the Start of the War on Terror* (New York: PublicAffairs, 2008), 65.

[72] See Rubin, 387, for his account of how this team continued to convene out of office to consider the financial issues of the day.

[73] Kevin Phillips, *Bad Money: Reckless Finance, Failed Politics, and the Global Crisis of American Capitalism* (New York: Viking, 2008), 59.

Chapter Three

Energy Security Is National Security

Keith W. Cooley

Defining national security can be a difficult undertaking because it can mean different things to different people. George Kennan has offered, in my mind, an uncomplicated but reasonable definition: "the continued ability of a country to pursue its internal life without serious interference."[1]

Over the years, the world has shrunk because of the many technological advances that have become commonplace (for example, the Internet, global positioning satellites, and electronic convergence), and with that shrinking, the context in which the term "national security" is defined has morphed. Forty years ago, no one would have thought it possible to be able to track someone's whereabouts using only a telephone (a phone represented a location, not a person, per se); the same holds true for the idea of stealing government secrets in the middle of the night while sitting in one's home thousands of miles away; and certainly few people would have believed that the survival of the species could be threatened by the thoughtless acquisition and use of carbon-laden fuels. Yet each of these concepts is now an everyday reality, and in their own way, they contribute to our personal and national feelings of insecurity.

Energy security can be described in many ways, but for the purposes of this chapter, to paraphrase the International Energy Association, we will simply call it "the assurance of the uninterrupted supply of energy at an affordable price, while respecting environmental concerns."[2]

We have seen energy insecurity growing at an alarming rate recently. From the ability of hackers to disrupt the flow of power on an international Internet-reliant grid; to the seemingly innocuous decision to make critical parts for energy distribution systems offshore, a decision that backfires the moment our supply base decides they are our competitors; to the growing threat to health and safety from oil spills and the environmental contamination it breeds: it is clear that ready access to cheap energy is becoming ever more problematic. When you factor in the uneven distribution of energy availability in countries across the globe and the manipulation of fuel pricing that threatens geopolitical stability, the problem becomes even more complex.

This chapter will address the notion of energy security as national security from four points of view that are, in my opinion, strategic priorities:

- Priority 4: widespread increased dependence on domestic energy efficiency

- Priority 3: migrating to alternative (sometimes called "clean") energy sources

- Priority 2: developing and sustaining an alternative energy capability

- Priority 1: creating strong civic, business, and political leadership to quickly implement needed changes that assure energy and national security for this country.

The Facts

Energy supply and demand play an increasingly vital role in our national security and the economic output of the country. It is not surprising that we spend more than $500 billion annually on energy.

The United States, on both domestic and military fronts, is a tremendous user of the world's proven supplies of energy. It is the world's second-largest consumer in total usage, at roughly 100 quadrillion British thermal units (BTUs)[3] annually of a 451-quadrillion BTU flow. Put differently, that means that 4.5 percent of the world's population uses 21 percent of the world's energy. For those who have traveled abroad, it is clear that energy is not only accessible, but also comparatively cheap. The majority of our fuels are petroleum-/oil-based (38 percent), followed by coal (23 percent) and natural gas (24 percent). Nuclear power provides 8 percent, and renewables weigh in at 7 percent.[4]

Moreover, our appetite for power and energy is continually growing. Facts pulled from a brutal but honest assessment by financier Michael Milken suggest an unsustainable (translate as "addictive") appetite for oil over the last 35 years (see table).

It is also clear that we are not the only substantial user of the world's energy supplies. In 2010, China overtook the United States as the world's largest energy consumer.[5]

Table. **U.S. Appetite for Energy**

Year	Foreign Oil Dependence (in percent)	Presidential Statement
1974	36.1	Richard Nixon: "At the end of this decade, in the year 1980, the United States will not be dependent on any other country for the energy we need."
1979	40.5	Jimmy Carter: "Beginning this moment, this nation will never use more foreign oil than we did in 1977—never."
1981	43.6	Ronald Reagan: "While conservation is worthy in itself, the best answer is to try to make us independent of outside sources to the greatest extent possible for our energy."
1995	49.8	Bill Clinton: "The nation's growing reliance on imports of oil . . . threatens the nation's security. . . . [We] will continue efforts to . . . enhance domestic energy production."
2006	65.5	George W. Bush: "Breakthroughs . . . will help us reach another great goal: to replace more than 75 percent of our oil imports from the Middle East by 2025."
2009	66.2	Barack Obama: "It will be the policy of my administration to reverse our dependence on foreign oil while building a new energy economy that will create millions of jobs."

Source: <www.businessinsider.com/look-who-failed-to-reduce-foreign-oil-dependence-2010-4>.

The facts are unambiguous. The United States:

- uses more of the world's energy resources than anyone else (except China)
- is using these resources at an ever-increasing rate
- is importing more of its energy supplies each year
- is in competition with our global neighbors for available proven reserves
- needs a cheap, readily accessible supply of energy to continue to thrive.

Clearly, strategies that lessen our dependence on traditional fuels from traditional sources are needed if we are to preserve our place in the global pecking order. So let us look at four strategic priorities that can greatly assist our efforts to have the energy we need when we need it AND to continue our role as a global leader.

Strategic Priority 4: Widespread Increased Reliance on Energy Efficiency

Energy efficiency simply means using *less* energy to produce the *same level* of energy service. For example, insulating a building allows the use of less heating and/or cooling energy to achieve and hold a comfortable temperature for its occupants. The use of fluorescent and natural lighting can in many circumstances provide as much or more light energy as a conventional incandescent light bulb. If there is any path that can quickly and easily move us toward greater energy security, it is energy efficiency.

A McKinsey and Company report titled "Unlocking Energy Efficiency in the U.S. Economy" states, in part, that "energy efficiency offers a vast, low cost energy resource for the U.S. economy—but only if the nation can craft a comprehensive and innovative approach to unlock it. . . . If executed at scale, a holistic approach would yield gross energy savings of up to $1.2 trillion."[6]

This $1.2 trillion savings on energy, which neither includes the transportation sector nor factors in the cost of greenhouse gas emissions, could cut the country's energy usage by as much as 23 percent (~ 9.1 quadrillion BTUs) by the year 2020. That would be more than enough to offset the expected growth in U.S. energy use if we continue at a "business as usual" pace.

Note that this savings comes from a $520 billion investment in energy efficiency improvements such as insulating basements, replacing old, inefficient appliances with newer ones, and sealing leaky building ducts.

With these energy savings comes the opportunity for consumers (whether commercial or residential) to take those same dollars previously used for energy generation and allow them to flow into other portions of the U.S. economy—for example, to offset costs of critical services like education and healthcare, as opposed to an economic model that sends many of those dollars overseas.

For the military, a comprehensive energy efficiency plan focusing on the warfighter would suggest, again, the ability to access the same level of energy services at a much lower energy cost. Lower energy costs in country may very well translate into lower fuel consumption.

Just as important is the notion that as the United States begins a serious effort to downsize its energy use, especially use that depletes precious fossil fuel reserves, more nations of the world will begin to see us as serious partners in the hunt for comprehensive solutions to global warming as well as to health hazards that arise from using oil, gasoline, diesel, and so forth. As that happens, the United States will find itself in better standing with countries that, in my opinion, now see us as addicted to energy at any cost. Their sense of us will change because of our significant efforts to commit to a more sustainable world through a change in perspective and behavior.

Strategic Priority 3: Migration to Alternative Energy Sources Leading to Less Dependence on Carbon-intensive Fossil Fuels

There are at least two significant reasons the United States must migrate from fossil fuels to alternative (sometimes called *clean*) sources (such as solar, wind, geothermal, and biomass) in the near future. Foremost is the fact that power generation by fossil fuels expels significant amounts of carbon into the atmosphere ($\sim$ 6.3 billion metric tons globally on an annual basis; see figure). This contributes to an ever-increasing global warming trend, 25 percent of which the United States is fully responsible for.

Experts believe the effects of this warming will be adverse, especially for the United States: "Likely future changes for the United States and surrounding coastal waters include more intense hurricanes with related increases in wind, rain, and storm surges . . . as well as drier conditions in the Southwest and Caribbean. These changes will affect human health, water supply, agriculture, coastal areas, and many other aspects of society and the natural environment."[8]

Moving to alternative fuel sources will greatly slow the rate at which we add to the problem because the amount of pollutants being put in the air will be reduced. That will be a huge step forward toward slowing, stopping, and eventually reversing global warming.

Second, as competition for these fuels increases, the cost to the United States in dollars and materiel (military equipment, apparatus,

Figure. **Global Carbon Cycle (in billion metric tons)**

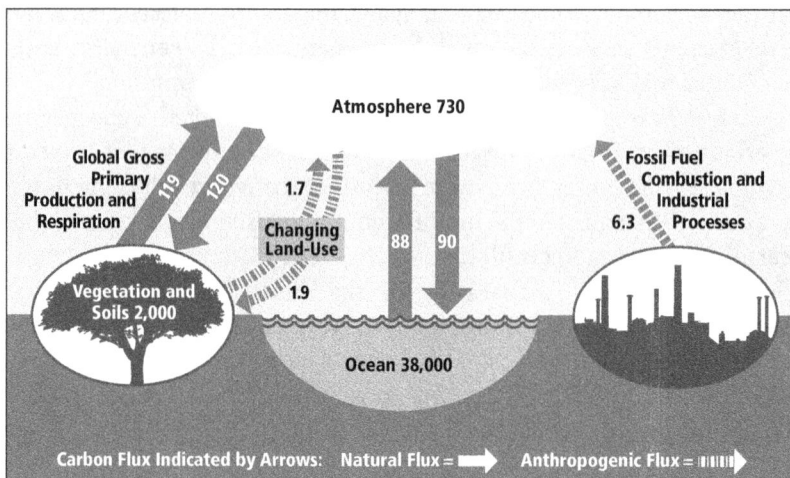

Source: Intergovernmental Panel on Climate Change, *Climate Change 2001: The Scientific Basis* (U.K., 2001).

supplies, and so forth) must increase, accompanied by a significant loss in global goodwill. China and India lead a contingent of emerging nations that will need more oil to sustain their rise in economic and military clout, and they will seek those resources from the same places we do: the Middle East (Iraq, Saudi Arabia), Africa (Nigeria), and South America (Venezuela). The United States, no doubt, will fight to keep its energy supply intact. On that subject, the following opinion was voiced: "Some countries such as the U.S. have enormous military expenditures in part to protect global oil areas for their interests. A number of other large countries are getting more involved or active in the international arena due to energy related concerns, including China and Russia prompting a fear of a geopolitical cold war centered around energy security."[9]

Moving to alternative fuels that significantly decrease our dependence on foreign-owned supplies will substantially reduce the level of competition in which we must engage to assure uninterrupted access to power and energy.

Of course, other reasons for making the transition are abundant:

- A "green economy" based on alternative energy will require a workforce skilled in "green jobs," an economy that will be associated with fewer health problems than that of our present energy/power generation industry and that will be built on "knowledge work." This suggests better paying high-tech jobs that will boost the U.S. economy and stabilize/raise the standard of living for millions of Americans.

- The sooner we make the changeover, the sooner we put the hurdles to such a change behind us, whether they are technological, process difficulties, consumer acceptance, or cost benefits of economies of scale.

- A smaller number of significant oil spills/leakages will occur (such as the BP/Deepwater Horizon mishap in the Gulf of Mexico in 2010) around the globe as these fuels become less important to satisfying our energy needs. Fewer spills mean fewer environmental concerns.

Clearly, then, moving to carbon-based fossil fuel alternatives for power and energy generation is an imperative if we are to overcome a series of key challenges to our present way of life.

Strategic Priority 2: Assuring that Alternative Energy Creation, Refinement, and Manufacturing Prowess Starts and Stays in the United States

Over the past 100 years, the American scientific, research, design, and manufacturing base has given the world thousands of technological advances from motorcars to spacecraft to cancer-fighting breakthroughs. Not only have many of these advances provided a better standard of living for much of the rest of the world, they also have given the United States a competitive global position second to none. However, that standing comes with a significant investment price tag.

A quick look at the numbers reveals that the Federal Government's investment has not been there: "The federal government spends less than 1 percent of its R&D budget on energy—a level less than one-fifth of expenditures in the 1970s and 1980s—clearly insufficient in light of coming challenges."[10] This is true not only in energy but also in most areas of scientific, technological, and manufacturing endeavor we would consider critical to our goal of self-sufficiency.

With that in mind, it should come as no surprise that the U.S. scientific/industrial base has been eroding over the past five decades, and our ability to continue to supply an ever-accelerating series of game-changing technical breakthroughs is heavily dependent on our commitment to such an effort—an investment in dollars as well as in the American creative spirit.

We must now focus our efforts on clean energy advances that improve existing technology while developing the "disruptive" proofs of concept that will lead us to the next level of energy/power generation and storage capability. We need this to happen in a number of areas if a comprehensive green future is to be realized. These advances include investments in power generation, energy storage, sustainable transportation, and smart grid technology, to name just a few.

At the same time, we will need to shore up our crumbling manufacturing base, which not long ago led the world in providing a host of products on a national and international basis. By that I mean the gears, bearings, advanced materials, and electronics that were the bedrock of manufacturing in the "old economy" and that will become the critical elements we need in years to come for wind turbines, solar cells, biomass gasification generators, and so forth to slow the pace of global warming. This will benefit not only us, but also residents of the entire world.

On the other hand, failure to embrace this course of action will lead to a loss of our global innovation leadership. That in turn will downgrade our status in the global pecking order with negative impact to our economy and a substantial downgrading of the American way of life *as we have known it*. Implicit in this loss is the notion that we will have to buy green products, for both domestic and military purposes, from others. From the viewpoint of national security interests, this is an unsafe place to be. The cost to the United States can certainly not be any less, and may be very much more, than the cost of investing in technological, scientific, and manufacturing leadership now.

Strategic Priority 1: Creating Strong Civic, Business, and Political Leadership to Quickly Implement Needed Changes that Assure U.S. Energy and National Security

I have made this the top priority because to me, it is the most important. The best plans in the world are little more than paper and ink unless they are acted upon. Unfortunately, we find ourselves in just such a circumstance. We have known for years how precarious our position has been. We know what we should do about it, and we know, at least in the short term, how to go about implementing the plans.

If we do, we can reduce and eventually stop global warming and the problems it could bring; we can lessen tensions between our global neighbors and ourselves that would otherwise grow because of the increased competition for a precious but diminishing natural resource (foreign oil); and we can revitalize the U.S. economy (built on alternative energy solutions), create needed green jobs, and rebuild a standard of living that was once foremost in the world. This work can start with the priorities discussed above.

Creating the collective will to make these changes will be a major undertaking requiring the attention and commitment of our nation's principal government, business, and community leaders. It will not be an easy task, but it is one that has been accomplished in many other parts of the world and, on a smaller scale, in the United States. It happens when opinion leaders in the community see the need for change and convince those in power, sometimes one person at a time, to commit to and lead initiatives that change the thinking and behavior of the community at large. Examples across the globe include China and Europe (wind and solar), Brazil (sugar cane ethanol), and projects in Seattle, Washington, Portland, Oregon, and Minneapolis-St. Paul, Minnesota (green jobs in weatherization/energy efficiency). America can take lessons from best practices in these locales and create a roadmap for national implementation.

This same collective will has been a part of U.S. history through-out the country's existence—most notably in the 1940s, when we saw President Franklin Roosevelt's "Arsenal of Democracy" quickly adapt Detroit auto production lines for the building of bombers, tanks, and guns; in the 1950s, when the creation of a national interstate highway system championed by President Dwight D. Eisenhower connected the Nation in a way not previously possible; and when the U.S./Soviet "space race" of the late 1950s and early 1960s was all but won by the realization of President John Kennedy's 1962 vision of having a man on the Moon by the end of the decade. We also will take lessons from these examples to realize the clean, environmentally sustainable, prosperous, and socially equitable future we all desire.

Conclusion

U.S. energy insecurity is growing as more countries of the world compete for a fixed (some would say diminishing) quantity of oil to satisfy growing energy appetites. This insecurity is worsened by the harmful effect that the burning of fossil fuels has on our atmo-sphere, exacerbating an already dangerous greenhouse gas problem that will negatively impact the rich, diverse environment of the Nation.

Overcoming these challenges starts with actions in the four specific areas outlined above (increased energy efficiency, increased clean energy use, assurance of a U.S. clean energy technical/manufacturing capability, and the will to act). Of all of these strategies, the most important one, and the one we have done the least to implement, is *moving to real action.*

We know what we need to do to increase U.S. energy efficiency. Energy audits to gauge need, installation of improved lighting systems and upgraded insulation, as well as the use of energy-efficient appliances are off-the-shelf strategies we can implement immediately. When paired with thoughtful growth planning, especially in urban areas and state-of-the-art Leadership in Energy and Environmental Design–sustainable building design, we can move the country to an increasingly smaller carbon footprint over the next few decades.

Mandating a national energy policy that calls for increased use of low carbon or carbon-free renewable energy sources can be done *now*, and the manufacturing of clean energy products in the United States for installation and use all over the country is feasible *now.*

The creation of a series of new U.S. energy research laboratories where innovative, disruptive concepts can be discovered, explored, and proven is within our means at this very moment. The ability to safeguard the intellectual property from these discoveries as well as the means to produce such products here in the United States is ours if we want it.

The creation of millions of new higher paying jobs driven by the demand for clean energy technology from entry level/green collar jobs to engineers and scientists can begin *now.* Those jobs can be shared by every segment in our society.

The question we must collectively answer as a nation is this: If we really want to remain in control of our own destiny, and if the means to do it are clearly at our disposal, why have we not done so?

I suspect the answer to that question is not an easy one, or if it is, it is not an easy one to hear. The answer may have to do with intestinal fortitude and the willingness to sacrifice short-term comfort for longer term/longer lasting gain. I also believe the answer to that question tells us a lot about our ability to act in unity for the good of the entire nation as opposed to the good of narrow-minded and somewhat insular interests. Whatever the case, those of us who understand the critical role energy security and environmental sustainability play in assuring national security have no other option but to endorse and encourage in the strongest ways the implementation of these priorities.

The comments made by Lou Glazier, head of Michigan Futures, when outlining the path forward for the state's economic revitalization are just as applicable for our nation:

> It's inconceivable to us that the big changes we are recommending can happen without *strong civic and business (and ultimately political) leadership*. If this project is going to avoid just sitting on the shelf, *there needs to be some group with clout that takes ownership of this agenda*. It is an essential ingredient in our future economic success.[11]

This chapter is written to urge action on energy security issues at the highest levels of government, industry, and civic engagement. We have many examples to draw lessons from both here and abroad that can inform our actions. But we must act; we must engage. It is the only path available for our survival.

Notes

[1] Robert E. Ebel, comments on the Economic and Security Implications of Recent Developments in the World Oil Market; before the United States Senate Committee on Governmental Affairs, Washington, DC, March 24, 2000.

[2] See <www.iea.org/subjectqueries/keyresult.asp?KEYWORD_ID=4103>.

[3] Wikipedia, World Energy Resources and Consumption, available at <http://en.wikipedia.org/wiki/Energy_in_the_United_States>.

[4] See <www.eia.doe.gov/aer/pecss_diagram.html>.

[5] See <www.iea.org/index_info.asp?id=1479)>.

[6] Kate Galbraith, "McKinsey Report Cites $1.2 Trillion in Potential Savings from Energy Efficiency," *The New York Times*, July 29, 2009, available at <http://green.blogs.nytimes.com/2009/07/29/mckinsey-report-cites-12-trillion-in-potential-savings-from-energy-efficiency/>.

[7] U.S. Department of Energy, available at <www.eia.doe.gov/oiaf/1605/ggccebro/chapter1.html>.

[8] Thomas R. Karl, Jerry M. Melillo, and Thomas C. Peterson, eds., *Global Climate Change Impacts in the United States* (Cambridge: Cambridge University Press, 2009).

[9] Anup Shah, "Energy Security," *Global Issues*, August 2010, available at <www.globalissues.org/article/595/energy-security>.

[10] James Duderstadt et al., *Energy Discovery-Innovation Institutes: A Step toward America's Energy Sustainability* (Washington, DC: Brookings Institution, February 1, 2009).

[11] Lou Glazier, "A New Agenda for a New Michigan," Michigan Futures, Inc., June 2006. Emphasis added.

Chapter Four

Achieving Energy Security That Feeds the Economic Component of National Security

Louis J. Infante

Energy has been and will remain an essential enabler of economic prosperity in the United States. Past prosperity was enabled by abundant and relatively low-cost energy and fuel. Even today, a majority of American citizens take our supply of affordable energy for granted. Without assured and secure sources of energy, our economy will be hard pressed to function normally and certainly will not be able to grow.

Having stated the obvious, the changes in the future of energy could not be more uncertain. The situation the United States faces is a critical one. The lack of a national energy policy and a robust plan for the future surety and security of our energy supply is hampering efforts to provide adequate and affordable forms of energy that fuel economic prosperity.

Why do we need a national energy policy and plan? Because after a number of false doomsday predictions regarding the eventuality of oil shortages, it is generally agreed that the combination of oil supply depletion and climate change effects will affect our economy for the next four decades. Many will say that much is being done to develop alternatives as we speak, and this is true. But the efforts are not coordinated and are not being planned with a view toward an overall long-term solution. Instead, short-term technology development and implementation are being installed without a real understanding of how they will affect the long-term goal of energy security in the 2030–2050 timeframe.

Should we not enact a robust energy scenario, the projected cost to the quality of life and overall political stability of the United States goes far beyond economic criteria. After decades of economic growth, Americans expect their quality of life, which has stalled over the last decade, to continue to improve. The political dissatisfaction we are now experiencing gives us an indication of a negative trend that could be exacerbated by an uncertain energy future. This dictates that we take a serious look at the energy issue quantitatively and understand the scenarios that can assure success. Our leaders need to see the complexity of the problem and potential future success scenarios in a way they can understand and recognize the costs of change and/or inaction when making decisions on future investments.

What is proposed is a National Energy Security Initiative. This initiative should be administered by the Department of Energy (DOE) and joined by every government department with responsibilities that will be affected by energy—in essence, practically all departments. In this initiative, a model of current energy use in the entire country would be developed. Then, a complex systems modeling exercise would map the changing technologies, use elements, and economic factors around the future potential scenarios. Policies and plans could then be recommended to deliver affordable and assured energy to all economic sectors and regions with future technology investments defined.

Current State of Affairs

The most influential dynamic affecting global distribution of energy demand is affluent population growth over the next two to three decades, which will result in a 30 to 40 percent increase in quantitative global demand (see figure). Fossil fuel discovery and supply will be stressed, creating shortages and pricing instability.

Figure. **Regional Shares in World Primary Energy Demand**

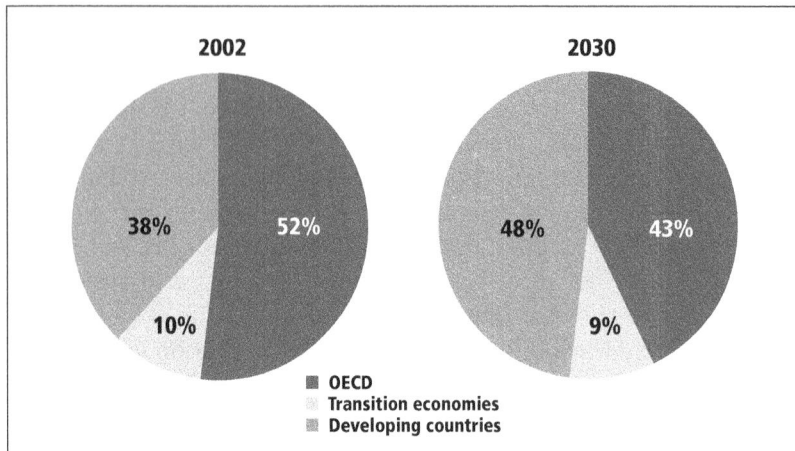

Source: World Energy Outlook 2004.

This is not the recipe for a future of energy stability in the United States. The landscape of supply and demand in fossil fuels will become chaotic. Compounding the problem is that the structure of the U.S. stationary power system is regionalized. As a result, we have multitudes of organizations and corporate entities with which to work. And now the United States is targeting the implementation of an electrified transportation sector. When all of these changing trends are evaluated in aggregate, the complexities do not allow for an intuitive understanding of policies and plans that are possible, affordable, and socially responsible.

There is an ocean of opportunity for technology development that will fuel technology exports. So our Federal Government has decided to invest in many different and competing research and development (R&D) programs. Without a national energy policy, the United States lacks any coherence of integrated effort or criteria on which to evaluate the research that is being conducted and funded.

There is no doubt that the Federal Government should continue to invest in forward leaning research. What is required here is to take all of this research and consolidate it into one modeling and planning environment to understand how the individual developments may contribute to a defined goal.

The Endgame

The vision for energy security of the United States is actually simple to qualitatively describe. It must be totally renewable; kind to our climate and environment; affordable; employ technologies that are not independently controlled by foreign interests; and create economic growth and jobs within industries that develop, deploy, and sustain it.

So how does that compare to what we have today? The United States is at best 15 percent renewable in stationary and 4 to 5 percent renewable in the transportation sector. We are the largest carbon dioxide producer in the world by a 5:1 factor. We are fairly affordable but subject to fluctuations that throw chaos into our economy on short notice. Foreign interests are dominant in the supply base, causing the majority of our negative balance of payments. Jobs are available in the energy sector but due to our declining development of technical professionals, some are filled by foreign students or are exported. This is a train wreck that may have already happened.

The endgame employs the following technologies:

- water flow technologies of hydro and tidal
- solar technologies of PV and CS
- nuclear (with fuel reclaiming)
- wind (all forms)
- geothermal generation
- H_2 (primarily for transportation)
- fuels from new forms of agriculture
- new, as yet undefined, renewable technologies.

The endgame includes the following characteristics:

- the basic technologies of energy generation and fuels are controlled by U.S. or allied interests
- new technologies, when integrated, will meet all supply and economic requirements
- the agricultural system will provide fuels and food without economically affecting either
- a new energy workforce will be trained in an education system that is coordinating its offerings to a national policy and plan and regionalized for local needs and advantages
- the technologies employed will be sustainable and not adverse to climatic or environmental elements
- the system will be affordable and contribute to the economic prosperity of the nation and its citizens.

An endeavor of this magnitude has succeeded before in the United States. The technological, educational, and organizational challenge of manned space flight to the Moon is on the order of magnitude of the complexity of the future energy state. We succeeded in that challenge and developed technologies that fueled the information age. These contributions initiated some of the building blocks that will facilitate our energy quest—computers, communications, and fuel cells, to name a few. This can be repeated in the new energy age.

Plotting the Path to the Endgame

The lack of a national energy policy, even though we are investing billions into R&D, leaves the United States in a situation described by the phrase, "If you don't know where you're going, any road will get you there." U.S. leadership must overcome barriers to establishment of a national policy on energy that prescribes an endgame and the plan to achieve it. Not doing so leads to variable outcomes, many of which can cause economic distress. Recognition of the need for the population to be educated to understand the changes that they will see and to have confidence that our leadership has the problem in hand is critical to political tranquility. And with the fossil fuel supply and demand curves spreading over the next 10 to 20 years, there will come a day when coordinated action will need to be organized. Rather than waiting until events such as the embargoes of the 1970s and the subsequent reactionary actions occur again, the United States should set policy, establish a clear course of action, and properly fund it. Most important is communicating with the American people to elicit wide-ranging support for the changes that will eventually come.

The path will be one of change, and it must have a significant amount of flexibility built into it. An example is the transportation sector, which touches most Americans daily. Over coming decades, cars will be powered by an expanding number of systems, from our current liquid fuels to hybrids to gaseous fuels and eventually electricity. The earliest possible conversion to a full electric-driven U.S. vehicle fleet is projected to be in about 35 years. Components of alternative transportation will be employed. Over this time period, people's transportation lives will change 3 to 5 times. This is a much higher rate of change to our population than any we have seen in our country's existence.

There is no easy fix to this and no single silver bullet to employ. The path will include the use of a number of interim solutions. Technology developments and validations will have variability in their deployment timelines. As technology is developed, it will have to be brought into widespread use, and certain elements may well have short life spans. But with a plan in place, the opportunity for success and economic security will be visible, whereas without a plan, success will only be a dream and the population will become frustrated. The energy world of 2030 will be a different one, and the United States is long overdue in setting adequate policy in this area.

A Way Forward

The proposal is to establish a National Energy Security Initiative. This effort should be established within DOE and include working elements from all of the Federal Departments that may be affected by or that may contain solution elements: Defense, Transportation, Agriculture, Homeland Security, and so forth.

The tasks within this initiative would be to:

- dynamically model the current energy use profile for the United States

- incorporate economic, sociological, educational, security, and political elements into the models

- develop the endgame models that incorporate all of the alternative technologies under development

- recommend to leadership a set of policies that will assure adequate energy availability as technologies mature

- monitor new and ongoing technology developments assessing their effect on the endgame and interim points

- communicate the needs, plans, and successes to the American people.

This approach can be tested and first implemented in a cross-department effort being created between the Department of Energy and Department of Defense (DOD) to provide for efficient and secure future energy usage in the latter. The modeling and planning can be exhibited to leadership within the DOD/DOE initiative. After initial investments, new systems can produce cost reduction and savings for the American people. It also sets an example by which the government itself is willing to embark on an organized planning exercise that can be tested and then expanded to include the entire country.

Conclusion

The energy profile for source and use will change drastically over the next 40 years. The next 20 years are the most critical for the United

States to position itself with assured and secure forms of energy. Considering the time needed to develop and implement significant reinvestment projects, we are already late in having policies and plans in place to forestall economic distress and all of its political consequences. The National Energy Security Initiative will provide the coordinating efforts in planning and technology R&D that can assure success in the redevelopment of the U.S. energy system. And it can start within DOD as a first application of success.

Chapter Five

A Well-educated Workforce: Vital Component of National and Economic Security

Myra Howze Shiplett, Wendy Russell, Anne M. Khademian, and Lenora Peters Gant

The world is awash in change. It is the truism of our times. President Barack Obama introduced his National Security Strategy with the following statement:

> Time and again in our Nation's history Americans have risen to meet—and to shape—moments of transition. This must be one of those moments. We live in times of sweeping change. . . . Our strategy starts by recognizing that our strength and influence abroad begin with steps at home. We must grow our economy and reduce our deficit. We must educate our children to compete in an age where knowledge is capital, and the market place is global.[1]

In May 2010, in a speech before the Council on Foreign Relations, Education Secretary Arne Duncan spoke of the importance of a well-educated citizenry: "America's success depends on the success of its individual citizens, just as the progress of humanity ultimately depends on the shared progress of nations. I believe that education has immeasurable power to promote growth and stability in the 21st century."

The history of the United States is replete with examples of the contribution of education to economic and national security. In 1635, less than 30 years after the first settlers landed on North American soil, the Boston Latin School was founded, and the first free school was established in Virginia. In 1636, Harvard College was established in Cambridge, Massachusetts, and in 1693, William and Mary College was founded in what is now Williamsburg, Virginia. In 1862, Congress passed the Morrill Act, which established "land grant" colleges:

> endowment, support, and maintenance of at least one college where the leading object shall be, without excluding

other scientific and classical studies and including military tactics, to teach such branches of learning as are related to agriculture and the mechanic arts, in order to promote the liberal and practical education of the industrial classes in the several pursuits and professions in life.[2]

By the last third of the 20th century, the citizenry of the United States was among the best educated in the world. In 2010, America was "ranked 12th in the number of 24- to 35-year-olds with college degrees . . . among 36 developed nations."[3] Discussing this issue before Congress last year, Gaston Caperton, president of the College Board, stated, "The growing educational deficit is no less a threat to our nation's long-term well being than the current fiscal crisis. . . . To improve our college completion rates, we must think 'P–16' and improve education from preschool through higher education."[4]

The College Board advocates achieving a 55 percent graduation rate by 2025 if America is to remain competitive with the rest of the world. This goal is in contrast to the 2008 graduation rate of just under 42 percent. To achieve the 55 percent goal, the United States must find a solution that supports college educations for low-income and minority populations within the country. Achieving this goal also assumes that progress can and will be made in getting children enrolled in preschool and elementary school and that they will stay in school through at least an associate's degree:

> According to OECD [Organisation for Economic Co-operation and Development] in 2007 our nation ranked sixth in post-secondary educational attainment in the world among 25- to 60-year-olds. The United States ranked fourth for post secondary attainment for citizens age 55–64. The United States trails the Russian Federation, Israel, and Canada in this age group. As America's aging and highly educated workforce moves into retirement, the nation will rely on young Americans to increase our standing in the world. However . . . among citizens between 25–34 in developed countries, the United States ranks 12th.[5]

In recognition of the inextricable link between national security and economic security, the National Defense University's August 2010 symposium entitled *Economic Security: Neglected Dimension of National Security?* examined various aspects of economic security, including the need for a well-educated workforce to drive the engines of creativity and economic growth. The human capital discussion panel took its text from President Obama's National Security Strategy:

> In a global economy of vastly increased mobility and interdependence, our own prosperity and leadership depends increasingly on our ability to provide our citizens with the education that they need to succeed, while attracting the premier human capital for our workforce. We must ensure that the most innovative ideas take root in America, while providing our people with the skills that they need to compete.[6]

The panel provided a variety of perspectives—from the importance of understanding the contribution of strategy, to an examination of the challenges currently facing the "P–16" educational system, to graduate education, and finally to the role and relationship between colleges and universities and the national security world of work.

America's High School Pipeline

Wendy Russell has devoted her professional life to educational reform. Her presentation offered insights to the educational challenges facing America. According to her, the Nation's critical national security human capital needs are threefold:

- candidates who are well versed in information technology (IT). Because this is estimated to be one of the top five Federal hiring requirements, that need will translate into 800,000 new IT hires by 2018.

- a diverse workforce that looks like the Nation

- increased supply of critical skills related to fluency in foreign languages and expertise in foreign cultures.[7]

The Federal Government spends between $70 billion and $80 billion each year on a wide variety of IT work, from design, implementation, and maintenance of enterprise-wide systems to assuring that individual employees have computers and support services needed for their jobs. Two out of three Federal agencies identify information technology as a mission-critical occupation: failure to have these capabilities in the workforce means that the organization will fail to accomplish its mission.

Against this background of need, the reality of today's high schools across much of America presents a very different picture. They still reflect the 1950s design of large, comprehensive schools serving as giant sorting machines for America's students: one track for those bound for college and professional careers, and another for those bound for agricultural and manufacturing jobs in the industrial economy—an economy that no longer exists.

There are 19,000 high schools in the United States that provide education to more than 15 million students. In a 2009 self-reporting survey, 95 percent of teachers stated they have computers in the class-room and that they use technology for instruction. Yet teachers also reported that their students' use of computers in the classroom during instructional time ranged from never (16 percent) to often (34 percent).[8]

Every year, over 1.2 million students—that is, 7,000 every school day—do not graduate from high school on time. Nationwide, only about 70 percent of students earn their high school diplomas. Among minority students, only 57.8 percent of Hispanic, 53.4 percent of African American, and 49.3 percent of American Indian and Alaska Native students in the United States graduate with a regular diploma, compared to 76.2 percent of white students and 80.2 percent of Asian Americans.

In a multinational world connected by technology and cheap and swift transportation to every corner of the globe, a world in which more than 6 billion people speak hundreds of languages and dialects, only 11 states have a 2-year foreign language requirement to meet high school graduation requirements. An additional five states require 2 years of foreign language for admission to the state university system, but not for high school graduation. Two additional states require 2 years for receipt of an advanced diploma, but not a regular diploma.[9] Many have proposals on the books but have tabled them for lack of funding.

A *Wall Street Journal* article reported that test scores for college entrance examinations have stagnated. Of the 1.6 million students who took the American College Testing examination, only 24 percent scored high enough in math, reading, English, and science to ensure they would pass entry-level college courses. This suggests that the core courses they are taking are not rigorous enough to prepare them for college or the workforce.

The price of providing remedial training is high. The Alliance for Excellent Education estimates the Nation loses $3.7 billion each year because students are not learning basic needed skills, including $1.4 billion spent to provide remedial education for students who have recently completed high school.[10] From the taxpayers' standpoint, remediation is paying for the same education twice.

The alliance estimates that if the 1.2 million high school dropouts from the Class of 2008 had earned their diplomas instead of dropping out, the U.S. economy would have seen an additional $319 billion in wages over these students' lifetimes. The alliance also estimates that the country could expect to lose well over $300 billion in potential earnings in 2009 as well, due to dropouts from the Class of 2008. If this annual pattern is allowed to continue, more than 12 million students will drop out of school during the next decade at a cost to the Nation of more than $3 trillion.[11]

It is these stark facts that led the Obama administration to say that the Nation's long-term prosperity depends on fixing its high schools and preparing students for the global economy, and to include the issues of a sound economy and a well-educated workforce as components of its national security strategy: "From unlocking the cures of tomorrow to creating clean energy industries, from growing our economy and creating jobs to securing our nation in the years to come, there is one constant in addressing these challenges: they all depend on having a highly educated workforce."[12]

Architecture of the High School Educational Future

Peter Smith's book, *Harnessing America's Wasted Talent*, states: "We have reached a tipping point in our educational and economic worlds, the point at which the needs for an informed and appropriately educated citizenry and the capacity to educate them have tipped away from the status quo, toward a future that must be invented quickly."[13]

Step 1: Know Your Customer

Know your customer, which in this case means know your learner. The Net Generation, Generation Y, or Millennials, born between 1978 and 1994, have grown up with technology. They are accustomed to group/team problemsolving. They are used to living in a 24/7 environment and expect constant high-tech stimulation. They want continuous feedback and recognition and flexibility in how they do their work.[14]

Step 2: Student-centric Technology

Schools need to create student-centric technology: a computer with software or online class time and subject matter chosen by the student. This approach—customizing material to how students learn—will clash with the need to standardize the way schools teach and test. Schools have done what all organizations do with new technologies: cramming them into existing structures, rather than allowing the disruptive technology to take root in a new model and grow, and then changing how they operate to adapt.[15]

Some encouraging activities are beginning in this regard, as the example below demonstrates:

> Over the past 10 years, many of California's high schools have gotten worse, according to the *San Francisco Chronicle*. In an encouraging trend, however, thousands of high schoolers across California have joined an educational approach called Linked Learning, which changes the way core academics are taught by combining classroom learning with real-world, work-based experience. The idea behind Linked Learning is simple: To make it easier for students to stay engaged, coursework must be relevant to their aspirations. For instance, at Skyline High School in Oakland, Calif., every 10th-grader chooses from seven different career-themed programs where they spend the next three years combining out-of-school internships in their academy field with a rigorous academic core, taught through the lens of their industry theme, which qualifies every student for college. Teachers are trained to incorporate this work-based experience into the classroom, and vice versa. In Skyline's architecture academy, for example, algebra and physics teachers show their students how the formulas they're learning are used in real-world projects like building bridges or designing buildings. The *Chronicle* describes one student, Cynthia Gutierrez, who entered high school "bored" and garnered mostly Cs and Ds her first year. In the 10th grade, she joined the education academy, centered on careers in education. "Before, I couldn't really connect with my teachers all that well," Gutierrez says. "But in the academy, it was different." Gutierrez's grades improved despite a more demanding course load, and have qualified her for admission to the state university system.[16]

A second example comes from a North Carolina school system. Elementary teachers in the Charlotte-Mecklenburg schools will be more effective at integrating engineering and technology in their science curriculum this year thanks to a curriculum developed by Boston's Museum of Science and local partners that include North Carolina State University, Discovery Place, University of North Carolina at Charlotte, and Duke Energy. Engineering Is Elementary (EIS) uses stories set in various places and cultures to introduce real-life engineering issues, as well as hands-on engineering design challenges that students tackle in groups. According to the Museum of Science, an estimated 1.2 million students in all 50 states will experience learning through EIS this new school year.

Step 3: Recognize the Learning Edges or Leverage Points

Milton Chen, a Senior Fellow of the George Lucas Educational Foundation, outlines innovations our schools need to employ in his book *Education Nation:*

Technology Leverage Point. From the Internet to mobile devices, online curricula and courses, technology-based content, platforms, and experiences are enabling students to learn more earlier.

Leverage of Time and Place. Learning can now truly be 24/7/365 rather than limited to what happens in a classroom 6 hours a day, 5 days a week, 31 weeks a year.

Leverage Point of Youth. Today's youth are becoming the first generation to carry powerful mobile devices wherever they go. These devices are used for instant access to information and their entire social network. This generation learns in a fundamentally different way, and it is teaching us how to restructure the educational system.

Step 4: Facilitate Seamless Transitions between Life, Work, and Credit/Degrees

We offer three examples:

- The California Institute for Regenerative Medicine has developed the country's first high school stem cell curriculum, which will be pitched to science teachers nationally soon and is already being taught at a handful of San Francisco Bay area high schools.

- In three high schools in Arlington County, Virginia (all included in the 100 top high schools in the country), German is taught in the learning lab by a university professor because student course enrollment at each school is not high enough to support a full-time German teacher paid by the district. The class is virtually linked to students in Germany with real-time conversations in German.

- The Westport, Connecticut, school district's math teachers decided to rewrite the algebra curriculum, limiting it to about half of the 90 concepts typically covered in a high school course in hopes of developing a deeper understanding of key topics. They replaced the math textbooks with their own custom-designed online curriculum; the lessons are written in Westport and then sent to a program in India to animate the algorithms and problem sets with animation and sounds.

Step 5: Interorganizational Collaboration

At the Economic Security Symposium, one speaker stated that two-thirds of science and technology innovations involve some kind of interorganizational collaboration. We must begin to employ innovative ways to serve those who have been underserved by traditional education methods. Now more than ever, it is critical that schools partner with universities and the national security, military, and intelligence communities to support Net Generation students as the U.S. economy shifts into a global marketplace, making education not a luxury but a necessity to remain competitive in the work force.

Another speaker, an expert in national security issues, challenged listeners to be aware of the "architecture of the future, to see across the categories to a comprehensive picture of how things relate." Many of our most advanced research laboratories are located in proximity to the Nation's struggling inner-city school systems—New York, Chicago, Los Angeles, and Atlanta, to name just a few. What if we were to link the military training technology that has generated breakthroughs in gaming systems, high-definition video, computer-generated graphics, augmented reality, and artificial intelligence with high school education programs to push the learning envelope?

America's leaders and parents must embrace the importance of connecting with students the way they want to connect to keep them engaged and learning.[17]

America's Graduate Education Pipeline

Dr. Anne Khademian spoke of the *pracademic*—the intersection of academic theory and the practical application of that theory to public policy—and of the effective development and implementation of public programs. She also focused on the fundamental issues of building collaborative capacity in public organization as well as the importance of building a robust, dedicated public service.

Graduate Education as a Pracademic Exercise

Traditional graduate education presumes that the student will spend 1 to 5 years or more on campus immersed in graduate-level classes and research. This model fits a number of students seeking graduate degrees, particularly those pursuing research, teaching, and scholarly occupations as their life's work. But there is another world, one populated by individuals who also seek graduate degrees but do not have the luxury of doing so, or who prefer to work and attend graduate school at the same time. They seek scholarly skills, knowledge, and insights but want to apply this knowledge in private and public institutions. For these individuals, a pracademic graduate education is the answer. Graduate education focused on the pracademic holds great potential for promoting the type of research and practical skills that are essential for engaging the most complex public policy issues. Strong graduate education can foster the collaborative and networking capacities essential for sophisticated research, policy development, and implementation, and can reinvigorate a professional commitment to public service informed by the institutional complexities and policy dynamics of the public arena. While graduate education takes on multiple forms at Virginia Technical University, the focus is on the scholarly development of graduate students as practitioners. These graduate students are often part time, but are deeply committed to growth as a scholar.

Here, the focus is on the full-time practitioner taking one or two classes per semester in a graduate program, usually several years after completing an undergraduate degree. Paul Posner and others have used the term *pracademic* to describe the practitioner/scholar. These individuals are primarily part-time students in the early to mid-career phase of life. They seek

> continuous engagement between the theoretical and abstract and the practical and real. Classroom settings combine the daily experience of leading, managing, and policy development with the theories of organizational dynamics, public policy processes, institutional characteristics, motivation, and so forth. The discussions are a continuous process of considering theoretical explanations in the context of daily experience. The benefit can be a more realistic grounding of research questions and scholarship, and a means to reconsider, reconceptualize, and reframe the organizational, policy, and leadership challenges of public policy.

Graduate Education Builds Conceptual Thinking and Critical Analysis

A centerpiece of graduate education, particularly in this context, is the emphasis on the capacity for conceptual thinking and critical analysis. The ability to pull back from the minutiae of the immediate and to see broader patterns, constraints, and influences on the policy process is vital for understanding the benefits of collaboration and the points of potential collaboration. The ability to question the accepted or to scrutinize options, whether theoretical or practical, in a systematic manner is central to graduate education, essential for working in collaborative settings, and essential in the emerging world of interagency collaboration and cooperation. In this world, agencies and their employees realize that lasting solutions to complex problems often require horizontal collaboration between and among multiple agencies.

Knowledge continues to increase at a rapid rate. Organizational and individual success often requires a deep, sophisticated knowledge of a field. Graduate education focused on the pracademic contributes to such knowledge. Whether for homeland security, national security, air traffic control, or any number of other fields of study, graduate education offers students the opportunity to dig deeply into the empirical dimensions of key public policy areas through their independent research or through course work.

The focus on collaborative skills for decisionmaking and consensus-building either contingently or longer term, critical analytic skills, and deep sophisticated knowledge of a field are essential components for leading within the complex policy arenas of today.

In policy arenas as complex as national security, homeland security, education, and the like, the stovepiped approaches to policy development and implementation no longer apply. As we have learned in the post-9/11 era, the capacity to share information, make decisions jointly, and deploy resources collectively and strategically requires the ability to lead collaboratively across different agencies, different jurisdictions, and even different countries.

Complexity requires collaboration and inclusion. This means:

- understanding multiple arenas, sectors, jurisdictions (deep knowledge)

- understanding the points of interaction, tensions, compatibilities (conceptual capacities)

- forging discussion, alternative ways of understanding problems, forging consensus (analytic capacities)

- decisionmaking (experience).

Two pertinent examples of this are President Obama's recently announced policy to eliminate homelessness in America within a decade and the work of the Project on National Security Reform whose goal is to achieve reform of the national security system.

Ending homelessness in America within a decade can only occur if multiple agencies collaborate and combine their talents and resources to tackle the complex and difficult set of issues that contribute to homelessness:

On June 22, the lead Cabinet secretaries from the United States Interagency Council on Homelessness (USICH), from the U.S. Departments of Housing and Urban Development, Labor, Health and Human Services, and Veterans Affairs joined Executive Director of the USICH Barbara Poppe to unveil and submit to the President and Congress the nation's first comprehensive strategy to prevent and end homelessness. . . . By combining permanent housing with

support services, federal, state, and local efforts have reduced the number of people who are chronically homeless
by one-third in the last five years.

The nonprofit organization Project on National Security Reform
also has identified interagency collaboration as an essential component
for assuring the Nation's security. In the global world, national security
means using all the elements of national power in acheiving a peaceful
world. This occurs not just as a result of military might, but also
requires a sound and vibrant economy, an educational system that
produces well-educated individuals who can think critically and
conceptualize alternatives, and a citizenry that understands the power of
assisting other nations in achieving economic and political goals.
Thus, those agencies involved in national security functions must work
together to assure that all the elements of national power are coordinated
to assure our country's security.

Building a Vibrant and Effective Public Service

Graduate education focused on the pracademic can also be
essential for rebuilding a professional commitment to public service,
which requires an understanding of the complexity of governance and
the challenges of governing. Graduate education can provide this deep
understanding. It also provides insight into the evolving role of government and agencies and the evolving relationship of government with the
private sector, with citizens, with contracting partners, and with other
nations of the world.

The challenges of accountability are central to effective and
efficient government. Accountability is a term everyone uses, but we
often cannot agree on what it might mean in practice. If we are to
govern in more collaborative ways, we will need more creative methods
of demonstrating accountability for joint and multipartner efforts,
including efforts to broaden and improve performance measurement.

There are also the challenges of governing to protect fundamental
values. All policymaking involves balancing priorities and preferences,
as well as balancing principles, such as security and privacy. Graduate
education focused on deep knowledge, conceptual capacity, and critical
analytic skills creates a foundation for engaging in this balancing effort
in an informed and meaningful way.

By challenging students to think deeply and broadly about the
complex issues of our times, graduate education provides a means to
strengthen the abilities of those in public service to analyze and identify

the root causes of problems and then to work collaboratively to fashion effective and efficient solutions to the problems at hand. This enhanced capacity to make government function better helps increase citizens' belief and faith in their government.

Results for Public Organizations

As this chapter has discussed and described, a well-educated workforce is essential for economic growth and for effective and efficient government. A real-life example of how these factors play out is found in the work of Dr. Lenora Peters Gant, who manages an academic outreach program for the Office of the Director of National Intelligence (ODNI) on behalf of the U.S. Intelligence Community (IC). Dr. Gant has built an academic outreach program that now extends to over 30 colleges and universities. Established in 2004, the Center of Academic Excellence (CAE) program in national security studies was created to support the IC need for multiple sources of well-educated young professionals to fill the many interesting and exciting professions in the community.

Unlike a lot of academic programs or partnerships that tend to emphasize immediate results, this program focuses on building long-term partnerships with colleges and universities in mission-critical occupations to help assure multiple sources of well-educated college graduates to work for intelligence agencies. This program, now in its seventh year, provides competitive grants to colleges and universities to encourage the development of curricula in a variety of scientific and technical areas, foreign languages, cultural immersion, and similar studies.

The program's goals are three-fold:

- to develop long-term academic partnerships with accredited colleges and universities that have diverse student populations and courses of academic study that align with the IC core skill requirements

- to provide financial and technical support to these educational institutions so they can shape curricula to meet specific IC needs

- to leverage and cultivate IC relationships with faculty and students of those institutions to ensure that the community has a diverse, highly qualified, and motivated applicant pool for its mission-critical occupations.

The program has six key strategic criteria and program components:

- IC-related curricula in core skills–related disciplines. CAE institutions must design, develop, and reshape curricula in disciplines that support IC mission-critical skills and competencies

- Foreign travel/study abroad/cultural immersion or awareness. CAE institutions must implement a competitive process and program to develop competencies in regional and international expertise, critical languages, and cultural awareness

- IC regional colloquium/seminar. CAE institutions must develop and host a National Security Colloquium in conjunction with consortium institutions in the institution's geographic area to promote awareness about IC mission, IC careers, value of public service, co-ops, internships, and opportunities for scholarships to study in IC-related fields

- Precollegiate and high school outreach. CAE institutions must develop and host high school outreach programs to attract talent to national security–related fields of study and promote awareness about the IC mission and functions

- National security–related research. As applicable, CAE institutions will conduct national security research in support of building intellectual capital in interdisciplinary fields of study, including the science, technology, engineering, and mathematics fields

- Mandatory reporting, assessment, and evaluation. CAE institutions must conduct assessments, track metrics to ensure return on investment, and report findings and linkages in accordance with ODNI guidance that focuses on an IC workforce prepared for 21st-century challenges.

The ODNI program has provided an additional benefit for the colleges, the students, and the Intelligence Community. It has served to educate students, professors, and other citizens about the functions of government generally and the Intelligence Community specifically. In a time when many citizens find their government complex and difficult to understand, this program made understanding the role and functions of government easier.

Conclusion

A vibrant, growing economy that provides jobs for America's citizens is an essential component of our national security. A critical success factor for such an economy is a well-educated workforce, equipped to deal with the complexities of the 21ˢᵗ century. We all have a stake in assuring that our children and our neighbor's children are well educated. The security of our nation demands this commitment.

Notes

[1] The White House, *National Security Strategy*, May 2010, available at <www.whitehouse.gov/sites/default/files/rss_viewer/national_security_strategy.pdf>.

[2] Edmund Sass, American Educational History Web site, available at <www.cloudnet.com/~edrbsass/educationhistorytimeline.html>.

[3] Tamar Levin, "Once a Leader, U.S. Lags in Attaining College Degrees," *The New York Times*, July 23, 2010.

[4] Ibid.

[5] John Michael Lee, Jr., and Anita Rawls, "The College Completion Agenda: 2010 Report," College Board Advocacy and Policy Center, 2010, 9.

[6] *National Security Strategy*.

[7] Wendy Russell, *Strategic Human Capital Plan* (Washington, DC: Office of the Director of National Intelligence, 2006); Viveck Kundra, *NetGeneration: Preparing for Change in the Federal Information Workforce* (Washington, DC: Chief information Officers Council, April 2010).

[8] Lucinda Gray, Nina Thomas, and Laurie Lewis, *Teachers' Use of Educational Technology in U.S. Public Schools: 2009* (Washington, DC: U.S. Department of Education, IES National Center on Education Statistics, May 2010), 6, 12.

[9] Janice Kittok and Ryan Wertz, "World Languages Graduation Requirements," National Council of State Supervisors for Languages, March 2010.

[10] Alliance for Excellent Education Web site, available at <www.all4ed.org/about_the_crisis>.

[11] Ibid.

[12] *National Security Strategy*.

[13] Peter Smith, *Harnessing America's Wasted Talent: A New Ecology of Learning* (San Francisco: Jossey Bass, 2010), 114.

[14] Anastasia Goodstein and Mike Dover, *The Net Generation "Dark Side": Myths and Realities of the Cohort in the Workplace and Marketplace* (Toronto: New Paradigm Learning Corporation, 2010), 19.

[15] Clayton M. Christensen. *Disrupting Class: How Disruptive Innovation Will Change the Way the World Learns* (New York: McGraw-Hill, 2008).

[16] James E. Canales, "Linking Courses to Careers Improves Grad Rate," *The San Francisco Chronicle*, July 25, 2010, available at <www.sfgate.com/cgi-bin/article.cgi?f=/c/a/2010/07/24/IN1K1EGR92.DTL#ixzz0uz2DMpfp>.

[17] Michael Jenkins, Vice President of Admissions and Marketing, Everest University Online.

Chapter Six

Innovation

Carmen Medina

In the 2010 National Security Strategy articulated by the Barack Obama administration, prosperity is identified as the second of four U.S. national interests. Specifically, the United States seeks a strong, innovative, and growing economy. Focusing on *innovative*, as it relates to economic security, the term *economic prosperity* is probably more appropriate. Innovation is appealing intellectually and psychically. Despite 32 years in the Intelligence Community, I have come to realize that my cognitive orientation is essentially a progressive one. I am much more interested in what can be than in what is.

We are living in one of those spurts of progress and innovation that punctuate human history on a fairly regular basis. I am inclined to believe the impact of the changes we are seeing now will have particularly profound—dare I say, unprecedented—consequences. For my purposes, it is enough that technological and process-based changes and improvements are bunching up right now like beach traffic on a beautiful Friday afternoon.

So how critical is it to our economic and national security for the United States to be an important driver of this innovation caravan? To answer that question adequately, there are four additional questions that must be explored.

1. How important is innovation to the overall economic health of the United States?

2. Where does the United States currently stand in the world's innovation index, and how are we vectoring?

3. How do our likely peer competitors compare to the United States in their innovation potential?

4. What is contributing to the conditions described in the answers to questions 2 and 3? What are the causes and correlates?

Using the approach of the so-called objective intelligence analyst in answering these questions, the following lays out what is known and not known about this topic, according to my view of reality.

Before proceeding to answer the questions, let us explore some definitions of *innovation*. The World Bank, in a recent report on agricultural innovation, defined it generally as neither science nor technology but as the application of knowledge of all types to achieve desired social and economic outcomes. Specifically, innovators master and implement the design and production of goods and services that are new to them and/or their societies.

People speak of many different types of innovation. The taxonomy of innovation is usually presented in the form of paired concepts that are in opposition to each other. So, for example, people speak of fundamental innovation, which is often technology-based and leads to new industries, as opposed to social innovation, which refers to changes in the way people behave. These changes in societal behavior—for example, most people adapting to cell phones or global positioning systems—are often essential to harvesting the advantages of fundamental innovations.

There is process-versus-product innovation; the experts generally agree that product innovation often creates jobs, but does it lead to a net increase in jobs? After all, new products usually displace the individuals working on the old products. Process innovation, however, usually eliminates jobs as few innovators seek to increase labor costs through process improvement.

Then there are several dual taxonomies that are generally describing similar qualities—the extent of change. Is the innovation revolutionary or evolutionary? This usually is assessed in terms of outcome. Is the innovation radical or incremental? This usually distinguishes ease of adaptation. Is the innovation continuous or discontinuous? This distinguishes those innovations that trigger mass extinctions from those that do not.

A final taxonomy pair distinguishes fundamental innovation from applied innovation. In this case, fundamental innovation involves science and engineering leading to a completely new paradigm, whereas applied innovations take these paradigm shifts and turn them into something utilitarian and, in some respects, pedestrian.

Now that the definitions are explored, let us return to the four questions originally asked. First, how important is innovation to the overall health of the U.S. economy?

Although some of the subsequent questions have less clear or authoritative answers, the facts here appear to be without controversy.

Everyone agrees that innovation has accounted for most U.S. economic prosperity in the post–World War II period. The Department of Commerce notes, for example, that technology innovation is linked to 75 percent of U.S. economic growth since the war.

Perhaps less appreciated is the unique role that venture capital and the modern private equity firm had in fueling post–World War II economic growth. It is generally agreed that the venture capital industry really began in the United States in 1946. There was private investment before then—the Transcontinental Railroad was a startup—but the investors were rich individuals acting on their own. This is a trend that the country appears to be returning to as the amounts required by startups decline precipitously as a result of Web services and cloud computing. Venture capital firms in the postwar environment began by investing in the new businesses started by returning veterans. This was a uniquely American concept at the onset, but Europe caught up by the 1990s.

Venture capital reached its highest percentage of gross domestic product (GDP) in the mid-1990s at just about 1 percent, but the cascading effects of venture capital are more significant. The National Venture Capital Association estimated in 2003 that ventured-backed companies were then providing more than 9 percent of all U.S. employment.

We do not have to take the lobbying group's word for it. The Organisation for Economic Co-operation and Development (OECD) estimates that in the United States, firms less than 5 years old have accounted for almost all of the new jobs created in the economy in the last 25 years. Put another way, established companies have essentially created no net new jobs during that same period. The Kaufman Foundation, in a recent study based on a new set of data from the government called Business Dynamic Statistics, analyzes that firms more than a year old actually have destroyed more than a million jobs net since 1977.

There does not appear to be a breakdown of exactly how these new jobs link to innovation, but many of the new firms every year are based on some type of innovation, whether it is fundamental, applied, or social.

The capacity for innovation has been the primary catalyst of U.S. economic growth. Indeed, capitalism essentially is built on innovation and the concept of creative destruction. Going forward, innovation will be even more critical to U.S. economic prosperity. And that is because our particular economic circumstances today imply that innovation not only will need to contribute to all U.S. economic growth but also will have the additional burden of compensating for antigrowth dynamics currently infecting the U.S. economy—specifically, the financial crisis and the necessary deleveraging taking place.

Economists agree that the hangover from a debt crisis is the worst kind of economic problem and lasts the longest, and this economic downturn is made worse by a simultaneous disruptive secular shift in the economy, from analog to digital. Unemployment will stay stubbornly high because companies are using this downturn to divest themselves of employees and occupations they no longer need in a digital and knowledge economy. There are some economists who have argued that a similar dynamic deepened the Great Depression, which was the occasion that finally allowed for the complete unwinding of the agrarian/horse economy that had dominated the United States during the 19th century. The only elegant way for the United States to resolve its deficit issues is to grow out of them. A nice average 5 percent per annum growth rate for the next 10 years might be a good place to start, but it will be unachievable without the frisson of significant innovation. It may be unachievable without a concurrent effort to reduce spending.

The mature nature of the U.S. population is another serious issue in this discussion. Although there is considerable difference of opinion among academics as to how population growth affects economic growth, particularly for underdeveloped and developing economies, most agree that the declining and aging populations of Western Europe and Japan necessarily cut into economic demand. The U.S. economy is not there, largely because of the positive impact of immigration, but we are also no longer going to benefit from the economic boost that was provided by the consumption patterns of the baby boomer generation.

So having established that innovation is critical to the future of the U.S. economy, let's turn to the question: how are we doing in terms of innovation—specifically, given the focus on national security, relative to other countries?

Measuring where countries stack up on an "innovation table" appears to have become a cottage industry in the last 10 years. There are two recent and credible studies that we can cite. A report compiled by the Boston Consulting Group and the National Association of Manufacturers that measures innovation inputs and outputs has the United States ranked eighth in the world. A second report by the Economist Intelligence Unit (EIU), sponsored by Cisco, has the United States ranked fourth.

These studies are not very exact or agreed upon. Although most people concur on what innovation inputs are, such as a skilled work force, education, research and development (R&D) expenditures, and so forth, innovation outputs are another matter. For example, the number of patents, a popular metric, is criticized by some who argue that patents only indicate inventions and societal concepts of intellectual property, not innovation.

It may not matter that Iceland or Switzerland is considered more innovative than the United States. Neither country will become a threat to national security any time soon. On the other hand, these studies underestimate where China is; the status quo always underestimates the "new kid on the block" because the status quo owns the yardsticks. That said, however, China's status as a holder of U.S. debt will be a strategic problem for the Nation long before China's innovation capacity. It should matter in the long term, of course, but by then China will be dealing with its own structural problems, such as the graying of its labor force.

There is, however, no doubt that the U.S. capacity for innovation has declined in relative and absolute terms over the last 20 years or so. Our standing has consistently declined. Other evidence points to a less vibrant American economy. For example, according to Deloitte's Center for the Edge, the rate of return of U.S. assets has declined by 75 percent since 1965.

How do our likely peer competitors compare to the United States in terms of their innovation potential? We have already discussed China's innovation performance and the methods of measurement that discount China's progress. According to these studies, other potential national security concerns for the United States, such as Russia, are essentially nonissues when it comes to economic innovation. Given its strong performance on pure scientific research, Russia retains the potential for military innovations, but its economy, which is dwarfed by China's in any case, is increasingly based on exploitation of natural resources and is not poised for strong growth or innovation.

The European Union (EU) and China are the two coherent economic powers that could deny the United States leadership—or a significant share—of the economic innovations that will shape the 21st century. But if Goldman Sachs was correct in recent projections, a broader trend, the emergence of the BRIC economies—those of Brazil, Russia, India, and China—will fundamentally alter the world economic map by 2020. Goldman Sachs may regret its inclusion of Russia in this list, given the developments of the last decade. The EIU, indeed, only speaks of the BIC. The Goldman Sachs report states:

> Our baseline projections, underpinned by demographics, a process of capital accumulation, and a process of productivity catchup, envisage that the BRICs, as an aggregate, will overtake the U.S. by 2018. In terms of the size of the economy, by 2020, Brazil will be larger than Italy. India and Russia will be individually larger than Spain, Canada, or Italy. By 2020 we expect the BRICs to account for a third of the global economy and contribute about 49 percent of global GDP growth.

Joseph Stalin said that quantity has a quality all its own. This kind of change in the global economy will have profound effects on the world that we in the West are inclined to not even want to think about. And it only serves to underscore the argument that U.S. economic prosperity depends upon our capacity for innovation; only innovation will allow us to fight above our weight class, that is, the absolute size of our economy—largely a function of demographics and maturity.

While many of the most innovative countries are in the EU, it is still hard to imagine the circumstances by which the EU would become a peer competitor for the United States, which returns us to China. Although China, in the EIU survey, is projected to rise to 50th in the Innovation Index by 2013, its low ranking is deceptive. China has risen 9 places in just 5 years, a rate faster than the EIU anticipated. In a separate study of innovation in BRIC economies published in *Research Technology Management*, it was noted that in 1995, China's patent count was the same as Brazil's. Now, it is seven times that of Brazil.

John Seely Brown and John Hagel, at the 2006 Davos conference, asserted that China is now the world leader in management innovation. The methodologies used to rate innovation by country are based, unavoidably, on how the West has done it and thus have a tendency not to appreciate how countries such as China, Brazil, and India might be doing things differently.

In theory, China's (or any other country's) success at innovation need not pose a problem for the United States. But it can affect U.S. economic capacity if U.S.-based multinationals choose to divert more of their R&D efforts to China, which is graduating scientists and engineers at an incredible rate. The United States is lagging badly on science, technology, engineering, and mathematics (STEM) education. If Chinese and Indian graduates stop wanting to work and live in the United States, our innovation potential suffers. By some estimates, Indian immigrants lead up to a third of the startups in Silicon Valley. Finally, the economic advantage of innovation, that of surplus income, goes to those who do it first and well. The more countries that have the skilled workforce and modern economic base for innovation, the harder it will be for the United States to be first to the pole.

Let me be clear here. I am not suggesting any malice or nefarious intent on the part of any other nation. These trends have impact regardless of the policies of specific governments. It is really just a matter of physics and arithmetic.

Why is the United States losing momentum in economic innovation? The literature presented several compelling reasons. We have already discussed one: falling behind in STEM education. Given the size of China's and India's populations, we will never be able to match them numerically, but at the rate we are going, the United States will simply be overwhelmed.

A second related issue is a current workforce that needs new training and skills.

A third reason is the inadequate U.S. Federal and state government support for an innovation-friendly environment. We lag behind many other parts of the world. For example, the United States ranks 17th among OECD countries in the generosity of its tax credits for R&D. France is four times more generous than the United States, according to the Information Technology and Innovation Foundation. This is not good.

A fourth factor points to the short-term perspective of too many U.S. companies and their outdated and myopic management/leadership concepts. Steve Denning, a leadership consultant, notes that the management principles of most U.S. companies are scalable bureaucracy. Bureaucracy is, of course, the natural predator of innovation. It appears that too many U.S. companies have become quite innovative in inventing ways to use fees to bolster their bottom lines rather than seeking to pioneer a new product or process.

Finally, it appears that the United States, as a society, culture, and economy, suffers from having transitioned into a status quo mentality. The public debate is about preserving what we have or returning to core values. Having been a student of dozens of countries over the last 30 years, I believe I can detect the difference in the vocabulary and body language of a nation looking forward versus that of a nation looking to preserve what it has.

Let me share some concluding personal opinions that you may find negative or positive, depending upon your perspective.

Innovation is our economic strong suit, but it will not solve all of the U.S. economic problems. It can create many jobs, but we are undergoing a significant transition in labor markets and the nature of jobs. It will not cure our debt problem.

As we transition from the knowledge economy to the creative economy, we are shifting away from economic concepts that can be captured in nationalistic or mercantilist terms. The Chinese are issuing statements and doctrine that suggest they do not quite believe this. National boundaries not only are irrelevant to knowledge and creativity, they also are actually counterproductive. Innovation is becoming more collaborative. So what do the terms *economic security* and *national security* mean, then?

We are focusing on security and spending on military matters out of proportion to our economic capability and economic potential. The experts tell us that our spending on healthcare is similarly out of proportion. In his seminal book *The Rise and Fall of the Great Powers*, Paul Kennedy argued that such disproportionate spending is an indicator of a declining great power. There is presumably an optimum balance between wealth creation and military strength. Are we there yet?

The conditions I have described are not a platform for continued U.S. "dominance" of the world. We do not want to talk about it, but the U.S. economy will not support single great-power dominance once our economy represents only about 10 percent of the world economy, versus the 50 percent it represented after World War II.

I always want to tell young people just starting their careers that their greatest challenge will be to help the United States make the adjustment from great-power status to a more complex but (I believe) still quite comfortable relationship with many peers. Our choice is clear: either we can not talk about reality and continue patterns of deficit spending that will only hasten a messy denouement, or we can begin to make the intelligent choices today that will ensure we remain the most influential society in the world even as we relinquish the status of sole superpower.

Conclusion

Sheila R. Ronis

The *Economic Security: Neglected Dimension of National Security?* conference explored the economic element of national power through the eyes of economists, industry, and government; expeditionary economics, energy security, the role of science, technology, research and development, and human capital. By the end of the conference, we hoped a framework would emerge that the Nation could use to develop a "grand strategy" for improving our economic viability. Systemic thinking should become the hallmark of a set of capabilities that should be used in the Executive Office of the President, perhaps in a Center for Strategic Analysis and Assessment, or within current infrastructure that already exists.

The economic element of national power is frequently neglected because the Nation does not develop grand strategy at all, which means that all of the grand strategies recommended at this conference have no means to be developed.

My involvement in this issue began about 20 years ago when, as a strategic management consultant to the private sector, I had an opportunity to do a little work with the U.S. Army War College in Carlisle, Pennsylvania. When I read the National Security Strategy for the first time, I assumed it was a subset of a larger national strategy. But I was wrong; the United States was not developing long-term, whole-of-government grand strategies.

As a strategic management professor and a systems scientist, I thought it was very odd that the private sector routinely used management tools such as forecasting, scenario-based planning, strategic visioning, political and economic risk assessments, and so on, but that our government, especially in a whole-of-government way, rarely, if ever, used such tools across the board—although sometimes, those tools were used in pockets, in specific agencies or departments, like the Intelligence Community, the State Department, the Department of Defense, or the Services.

What mechanisms should the government develop to improve the Nation's ability to plan in a whole-of-government way for a future that will be very different from its past and that needs nonlinear systemic approaches to problem-solving using both analysis and synthesis?

To be successful in addressing a complex system, we need to integrate all major elements of national power: diplomatic, informational, military, economic, and so on. When successfully combined, our vitality as a nation is ensured, and our ability to encourage positive change throughout the globe is enhanced.

As a complex adaptive system, the future national security system will need to possess certain inherent qualities that will be critical to success. It must:

- share information and collaborate horizontally
- accommodate unanticipated needs and partnerships
- ensure agility in the face of uncertainty
- incorporate ad hoc structures and processes
- maintain a long-term view.

Because we are talking about complex adaptive systems, it is difficult to separate geopolitical, social, and economic phenomena. We tend to see all these elements interacting as a system of systems. In fact, in most instances, we are viewing complex systems of complex systems, and that is the challenge we all face.

Globalization has resulted in a world that is increasingly interconnected and interdependent. Readily available technology, environmental degradation, global capital market collapses, transnational terror, global disease, cyber attacks, and a host of other concerns have added complexity to the national security landscape. This environment will demand the application of a wide range of traditional and innovative strategies and tactics to counter threats and take advantage of opportunities.

Based upon both the realities we face today and the context emerging for tomorrow, let me make a few basic observations.

First, *the world is a system*, like a spider web. Movement or damage in one spot has the potential to be felt throughout the entire web. While the ripples in a pond may be visible closest to where the stone is thrown, the entire pond experiences some level of movement and/or impact. Global interdependence is now a reality, and national security and economy issues must always assume a global focus.

Second, *our homelands are no longer protected by distance or time*. The great oceans that buffered the United States from much of the world, for example, no longer serve as boundaries. Therefore, the distinction between foreign affairs and homeland concerns has become blurred—perhaps even nonexistent. Economic security is a merged mass of internal, external, and interdependency issues, and this has enormous consequences.

Third, *the reality of globalization demands a holistic worldview* alongside of our specific national interests. The needs and concerns of every country must be developed in concert with the welfare and security of the entire globe. To participate in globalization requires new ways of connecting to everyone else on the planet to ensure we are all secure; a rogue nation or rogue citizens can change everything in far-reaching ways.

More than 2,500 years ago, Chinese philosopher Sun Tzu said in his masterpiece, *The Art of War*, "If you know your enemy and you know yourself, you need not fear the result of a hundred battles. If you know yourself but not the enemy, for every victory gained, you will suffer a defeat. But if you know neither yourself nor the enemy, you will succumb in every battle."

What this quotation says to me in today's context is if you are in any kind of economic competition, you must be familiar with, and develop knowledge of, your competitors as well as yourself if you expect to be successful. How well have we developed relationships with all of our partners and friends to ensure we can cooperate when we have a problem anywhere on the globe? No one is big enough to truly cover the globe in terms of knowledge and/or capabilities. And think of the ramifications of this to a global economy of interdependencies.

General Dwight D. Eisenhower, as the Supreme Allied Commander in Europe in World War II, said, "The plan is nothing, planning is everything." Through the knowledge gained in the planning, we are able to more successfully enact the plan. And this is learning about the system in the Sun Tzu sense.

Thinking about the complex systems the national security community is dealing with, the physicist in me knows that understanding the characteristics of those complex systems is critical. Probably the most important characteristic we need to remember about complex systems is that they can rarely be controlled and at best can be influenced. And we can only influence those complex systems if we understand them intimately—if we have what the great American statistician W. Edwards Deming called "profound knowledge."

In the national security community, we are always being asked to make predictions. But predictions assume theories, and theories require assumption testing to learn. The complexity sciences say that in complex systems, there are limits to what we can learn or know with any precision; we can predict with probability but not with certainty. Even in physics, the Heisenberg Uncertainty Principle tells us we may not always be able to predict everything; if we know some things, we cannot know other things. Such is the case in the national security system, including the economies that we are trying to influence.

I find it interesting that the policymakers we work for and the bureaucracies we serve are not populated with knowledgeable leaders on this particular subject. They want us to predict and control the real-world complex systems we are supporting. And, of course, we know that we cannot do that.

Working in the world of complex systems, which is the real world of national security, requires planning and learning. And the more planning and learning we do, the more successful our capabilities in foresight, designing, developing, and ultimately protecting the complex systems we need for the future.

One of the Vision Working Group findings in the Project on National Security Reform includes the need to synthesize "all-of-government" and sometimes "all-of-society" solutions to complex system issues and problems. The only successful way to do that is to be learning about the system issues—in hyper-learning modes using accelerated learning processes and coupling those with foresight tools such as the Delphi technique used in the project to "stress test" its findings to Congress. These enable the development of scenarios for planning and ultimately developing grand strategies.

We also found that the United States needs to systematically use these tools and processes to improve decisionmaking, and we found we do not have mechanisms in place for that to happen at the whole-of-government level—at the level of the President.

For that reason, we recommended the establishment of a set of capabilities in the Executive Office of the President that would be in the business of developing scenarios and grand strategies to apply lessons learned in a world of complexities. And that requires context, analysis, and synthesis. It also requires breaking down the stovepipes of government so they can work together because the United States never seems to be ready when it needs to be. Contingency planning outside of the military is rare indeed! We need to create the mechanisms to use complex systems thinking and foresight tools in the decisionmaking processes of the executive branch of our government. And I suspect we will need to use strategic thinking if together, as a community, we hope to be successful in creating a world that is peaceful, secure, and prosperous.

There are two strategic weaknesses of the United States that regularly keep us from looking at our future in a strategic and systemic way and preparing ourselves for that future. We do not engage in strategic visioning or foresight exercises, and we do not write and/or execute grand strategies *as a nation*—and we need to do both.

First, we need to establish the planning and foresight capabilities within the interagency process that will continuously develop scenarios of the future to help senior government policymakers plan for an integrated future across the entire government spectrum, including Congress. This will probably include congressional committee reform that creates interagency mission funding and oversight mechanisms through inter-committee decisionmaking processes across jurisdictional boundaries. Systems scientists see the need to break down the barriers in the stovepipes of government from top to bottom. And finally, we need to help senior government policymakers plan for the future and the role the United States will play in it, including how we will remain strong in the George C. Marshall sense: remaining strong to maintain the peace.

As a nation, we need to become proactive in shaping the future of the world and working toward a future of increasing liberty, prosperity, justice, and peace because that is the world we want our children and grandchildren to inherit. We need to ensure we have a sound economy, or they will have no jobs.

I think that improving the foresight and planning capabilities within the Executive Office of the President will improve decisionmaking processes so that the Federal Government can be more effective in ensuring the Nation's future is better, freer, and more secure than the past. The entire world expects the United States to remain a leader. We cannot do this unless we are strong. And we cannot be strong unless we plan for and shape our future as a Nation with a sound economy.

About the Contributors

Editor

Sheila R. Ronis is Director of the Master of Business Administration/Master of Management Programs at Walsh College. She is also President of The University Group, Inc., a management consulting firm and think tank specializing in strategic management, visioning, national security, and public policy. Dr. Ronis chairs the Vision Working Group of the Project on National Security Reform (PNSR) in Washington, DC, which has been tasked by Congress to rewrite the National Security Act of 1947. As a Distinguished Fellow at PNSR, Dr. Ronis is responsible for the plan and processes to develop the Center for Strategic Analysis and Assessment, where the President will conduct grand strategy on behalf of the Nation. Dr. Ronis holds Master's and doctoral degrees in large social system behavior from The Ohio State University.

Contributors

Keith W. Cooley is Chief Executive Officer (CEO) of the advisory firm Principia, LLC. He previously was President and CEO of NextEnergy, an accelerator for alternative energy businesses and technologies, where he led the creation of a robust sustainability plan and helped the organization reconnect to vital funding from the foundation community. Prior to joining NextEnergy, Cooley was the Director of the Department of Labor and Economic Growth and a Cabinet Member to the Governor of Michigan. Mr. Cooley's background includes work as an experimental physicist, engineering program manager, strategic planner, and CEO of Focus: HOPE, where he championed the organization's work in manufacturing technology and workforce development serving underrepresented urban youth.

Lenora Peters Gant is the Deputy Associate Director of National Intelligence, Human Capital, for the Intelligence Community (IC) and the Director of the Office of the Director of National Intelligence IC Strategic Mission Outreach. Dr. Gant oversees the Intelligence Community's Center of Academic Excellence programs at 30 accredited U.S. colleges and universities. Prior assignments included Senior Advisor and Special Assistant to the Director of Central Intelligence (DCI) and the

Deputy DCI for Community Management about workforce management, training/education, human resources, and IC corporate diversity management. Dr. Gant holds a Master of Arts degree from Vanderbilt University and a Ph.D. from Virginia Polytechnic Institute and State University.

Louis J. Infante is the Executive Director, Government and Military, for Ricardo, Inc., an independent automotive engineering consulting company, where he is responsible for strategy development and enactment in the military and government markets. Prior to joining Ricardo, Infante served as Executive Vice President for McLaren Performance Technologies and as Chief Operating Officer of one of their business units. Other assignments include Managing Director for A.G. Simpson/Usiminas LTDA in Sao Paulo, Brazil, Vice President at APX International, and 13 years in engineering and manufacturing positions at General Motors and Chrysler. Infante holds a Bachelor of Science degree in automotive mechanical engineering from Kettering University.

Anne M. Khademian is Program Director for the Center for Public Administration and Policy at Virginia Tech in Alexandria, VA. She is also the co-convener of the center's Leadership and Administration Round Table series, featuring public leaders and leadership scholars focused on the challenges of leadership in public administration. In 2009, Professor Khademian became a Fellow with the National Academy of Public Administration. Before joining Virginia Tech, Professor Khademian taught at the University of Wisconsin, Madison, the University of Michigan, and the University of Pennsylvania. She is a co-editor for the *Journal of Public Administration Research and Theory* and a member of several editorial boards, including *Public Administration Review*.

Carmen Medina retired from the Central Intelligence Agency (CIA) in February 2010 after over 30 years of service. Her last assignment was as Director of the Center for the Study of Intelligence (CSI), where she developed and managed CIA's first agency-wide Lessons Learned Program. From 2005 through 2007, she was the Deputy Director for Intelligence, a member of the executive team that led the CIA's analytic directorate. Earlier in her career, Ms. Medina was Chief of the Strategic Assessments Group in the Office of Transnational Issues, Directorate of Intelligence. She graduated from Catholic University with a Bachelor of Arts degree in comparative government and pursued graduate studies at Georgetown University's School of Foreign Service.

John F. Morton is a Distinguished Fellow and the Homeland Security Lead for the Project on National Security Reform. He is also the Strategic Advisor to DomesticPreparedness.com and a consultant to Gryphon Technologies. With over 25 years of experience in complex national and homeland security issues, he has consulted and conducted independent research and analyses for BAE Systems/Detica, Technology Strategies and Alliances, Lockheed Martin Government Electronics Group, United Defense, L.P., Business Executives for National Security, Forecast International/DMS, Center for Strategic and International Studies, and National Defense Industrial Association. Mr. Morton has been extensively published and has written for almost every major defense publication.

Wendy Russell has spent 20 years serving the education and leadership development communities in the United States and Latin America. She helps create and facilitate arenas where adults and youth learn and gain leadership savvy and helps them apply those new skills. Her work supports educators, leaders, and volunteers. She is the author of *Preparing Collaborative Leaders: A Facilitator's Guide* (Institute for Educational Leadership, 1994) and has served at American University, the Institute for Educational Leadership, and RMC Research. Ms. Russell has a Bachelor of Arts degree in political science from the University of Tennessee and a Master of Arts degree in international education from American University.

Myra Howze Shiplett is President of RandolphMorgan Consulting LLC. She has advised a variety of governments, nonprofit organizations, and private sector firms on organizational effectiveness and human capital management issues, including work on the Project on National Security Reform and Ukraine judicial reform. She is also currently serving as international public service reform expert for the Government of Iraq. Prior to forming her own consulting firm, Ms. Shiplett directed the National Academy of Public Administration's Center for Human Resources Management. Ms. Shiplett spent more than 30 years working for both the executive and judicial branches of the Federal Government. She holds a Bachelor of Arts Degree in English and journalism from the University of South Florida and a Master's Degree in urban affairs from the Virginia Polytechnic Institute and State University.

David M. Walker is President and Chief Executive Officer of the Peter G. Peterson Foundation. In this capacity, he leads the foundation's efforts to promote Federal financial responsibility and accountability today in order to create more opportunity tomorrow. Previously, Mr. Walker served as the seventh Comptroller General of the United States and as head of the U.S. Government Accountability Office for almost 10 years. He also has over 20 years of private sector experience, including approximately 10 years as a Partner and Global Managing Director of Human Capital Services for Arthur Andersen, LLP. During this period, he also served as one of the two Public Trustees for Social Security and Medicare. A frequent writer and commentator, Mr. Walker has authored three books and is a subject of the critically acclaimed documentary *I.O.U.S.A.*

www.ingramcontent.com/pod-product-compliance
Lightning Source LLC
Chambersburg PA
CBHW080206300326
41934CB00038B/3391